How Can I
INCREASE
the
VALUE
of My
BUSINESS?

Turn Your Business Valuation Into A Value-Building Blueprint

The Expert Answer From
Richard Mowrey

Published by: Groundhog New Media

ISBN: 978-0-9978801-4-4

Version 2020.01.28

Cover Design by 100Covers.com
Interior Design by FormattedBooks.com

HOW CAN I INCREASE THE VALUE OF MY BUSINESS?

"Rich Mowrey has done it again. He is taking complex ideas related to selling a business and turning them into practical tools for the business owner looking to reap the maximum value from their life's work. Rich makes it clear that early and regular valuation reports give every owner the up-to-date roadmaps to turn the dials to maximize profit and efficiency along the way. Every business owner will find this book a life-saver."

DENISE LOGAN,
THE SELLER WHISPERER,
AUTHOR OF THE SELLER'S JOURNEY

"Mr. Mowrey uses his proven expertise as he lays out how to make your valuation work for you. This book's message is clear. To grow the value of your business, start with the vision that a valuation provides. You can then use its findings to guide your steps forward!"

JOHN C. JOHNSON,
MANAGING PARTNER,
IBG BUSINESS / BLUESTEMUSA

"Whether you're just starting out or you are already the owner of an established business, Rich Mowrey's new book, *How Can I Increase the Value of my Business?*, contains the clear, straightforward advice and tools that you need to ensure you capture the most value when it's time to relinquish your business. Make this book and its advice part of your regular planning process—your business and family can only benefit!"

CYNTHIA WAISNER,
PH.D., OWNER AND CO-FOUNDER,
CATALYST CONSULTING PARTNERS, LLC.

"*How Can I Increase the Value of My Business?* is highly recommended for business owners and their advisors. Owners' should discuss with their accounting team how the valuation concepts described in this book can help to focus management's analysis of operations on the correctness of the balance sheet accounts, the speed to liquidity of customer transactions, and the conversion of revenues into EBITDA. This book is an easy read that can lead a management team into a fundamental organizational transformation to be more value centric."

JOHN M. KRIAK,
FINANCIAL COACHING AND STRATEGIC CONSULTING,
GROUPGENESIS, LLC

WHEN THAT DAY ARRIVES TO TRANSFER THE OWNERSHIP OF YOUR BUSINESS.

YOU DO NOT WANT TO BE SURPRISED!

Some new knowledge coupled with your actions will help make sure that never happens!

USE the FREE
Ultimate Planning Checklist
To gain some personal momentum today!

To gain access, please visit:

https://www.mergermentor.com/public/
Check-List-To-begin-a-personal-planning-process.cfm

CONTENTS

INTRODUCTION

IF YOU OWN a business, this book is for you! The definition of a "business owner" that captures the breadth of responsibility involved is this:

"An individual or entity who owns a business in an attempt to profit from the successful operations of the company's collection of assets and processes. A business owner has final decision-making abilities and is accountable to maximize the overall value of the deliverable results."

Most business owners are not familiar with the business valuation process. Even fewer know how to maximize the benefits from the myriad of information within a valuation report. This is true primarily, because they have no driving business reasons to seek such understanding. This is a fact because, all too often a valuation (appraisal), is developed for a specific purpose outside the operating business.

The "typical" report may be part of a divorce settlement or an estate filing. Consequently, most of the focus will be on the resulting estimate of value and not on all of the important research and other useful materials that can be found within the report.

The REAL VALUE that can be gleaned from a valuation report goes far beyond the specific value estimate for the business. This book takes a look at how reports are developed and at the contents of the report from an "action-oriented" point of view. In that way, business owners will be provided the tools and knowledge to gain significantly from a valuation of their business. This is the step that each enlightened business owner can take to get a lot of "real value" directly from immediate and future uses of a business valuation report.

This book was specifically prepared to alert all business owners to the reality that there is an ocean of critical planning information to be found in each properly prepared business valuation (appraisal) report.

This external and internal information found to varying degrees and forms in business valuation reports, properly recognized, can be used to improve operating outcomes, increase the value of the business, and to improve the overall transferability of the entity.

Fortunately, <u>more valuations are now being prepared for use as important inputs to planning</u>. This is a use that can be very important over the long term. *(Not that the establishment of estate or buy-sell values, or in divorce actions are not important when needed.)* Use of the contents of a valuation report can be powerful in the hands of a knowledgeable business owners and his/her advisors. This specific actionable intelligence can be identified within a typical valuation report.

The objective of this book is to provide an overview of what the valuation analysts do in preparing a report. Why they do what they do and their thinking to point out how a business owner can use the available information and attendant insights. As part of this effort, recommended uses of such information, to increase the long-term growth of value, will be shown in detail within a simplified "example company."

As you (a business owner) read and hopefully reread parts of this book, please look for what will impact the value of your business over time. This process will advance your ability to develop the plans and to take the actions that will make the biggest difference, not only in value improvements, but in the joy of managing a growing business both in the near-term ... and the long-term.

A BUSINESS VALUATION is a fundamental tool that every business owner can and should use to measure and manage value. Understanding what affects the value of your business is required to react to external changes and to effectively increase the value of your business in preparation for that "someday" business ownership transfer.

One way to approach the information and the benefits that you can develop from this book is to think of a business valuation as follows:

A business valuation (appraisal) report for your business, in the very simplest terms, is a story about the history, the current position, and the future prospects of your company. You, as the business owner, are the creator of this story ... (past, present, and future) ... as it is ultimately reflected in the valuation report.

A quick look at the business ownership landscape will highlight the need to think ahead and to learn as much as possible to protect and enhance the value of your business. This dive into the overall situations in which a focus on business value becomes increasingly important should provide some perspective. It will also help you sufficiently appreciate what is involved in the entire valuation process. This mindset will help you put the knowledge gained to optimal use.

There are some interesting statistics that, unfortunately, are not widely known. Almost all business owners believe that they can address the "transfer of ownership somewhere down the road" when they decide it is time to seek a change of ownership! All too often they wait until it's too late and then they're disappointed in the results they must accept!

Here are three (3) sets of stats to consider:

1. Statistics show that <u>50 percent to 80 percent of business owners do not know the value of their businesses</u>.
2. Over 90 percent of owners do not formally or informally manage value.
3. **Most owners of privately held businesses have <u>over 80 percent of their net worth in their business.</u>**

This is IMPORTANT! When you combine these statistics, you can see the need for emphasizing a focus on value in this business area. A lack of working knowledge on value creation can lead to both poor operations performance and poor prices and terms in transactions!

Only one in three businesses in the lower middle market *(businesses with revenues between five and a hundred millions dollars)* and only one of six in the general business market *(businesses with revenues less than five million dollars)* actually close a planned transaction.

Only 1 of 3 Sell

The reason is twofold:

1. A lack of value management causes poor timing
2. Poor price expectations

The second is the number one reason why deals do not close.

A business valuation, because it measures current value, can become an essential management tool to use to place attention on value improvement over time. A valuation provides reference data and analysis for use in planning changes to affect future value. The term that is often used to describe this key management function is: Value Engineering.

My definition of *value engineering* is this:

> **Value engineering for a business entity is an application of a systematic method or methods to improve the value of products, goods, or services by the examination of the business functions.**

The key word in the definition is "examination," which is an investigation based on carefully developed information. It is the output from the "examination" of the business that yields an abundance of useful materials as inputs to plans and actions. This book will take a look into how a business valuation is developed. This should help you fully appreciate what is involved and how to put the available "working intelligence" (your new personal knowledge of the value drivers within your business) to better and better use.

If you have not had a business valuation developed for your business and you are asking yourself, What should I do?, the answer is to find the right professional who will provide you with the benefits outlined in this book. And ... then to consider engaging that same valuator to provide you with a periodic update.

Take a step back and think of when you might have done something like this. By revealing unrealistic expectations you can avoid this problem. Unfortunately, this is the final chapter of the story for too many business owners.

Improving performance is critical for gaining a good result. Timing based on industry and market knowledge often makes a notable difference. Your advisors can help in this area. More and more businesses are adding outside directors as one small step to broaden inputs of this nature.

A valuation provides reference information and analysis for use in planning changes to affect future value *(i.e. to write the best possible "story" of your business)*.

A business valuation is very much like a blood test before surgery. None of us would go into a surgery without a full battery of tests. The surgeon uses the testing knowledge to specifically make positive changes in the action he or she will take.

A business valuation is just such a group of tests. Tests that can and will help develop an effective strategy to build out a more successful business. A reflection on the company's strengths and weaknesses help a business owner create a more valuable business, one that will be more fun to manage and is better positioned to grow in value.

One thing that is more important than the direct value measure is the newly identified operational improvements that impact margins and cash flow. The company and industry research that yields these insights are key elements in any properly prepared business valuation. That is why many professionals believe the best and highest use for a valuation is in strategy development and in the annual planning process.

Every business owner expects to someday transfer the ownership of their business. Those plans and the related decision seem to be far into the future for most owners. Those dates in your planning calendar are closer than you think!

Prepare for the Dismal D's

The problem is that all owners are subject to what leading estate planners call the Dismal D's. (Divorce, Disability, Death, and Distress within the business) These are the unplanned occurrences that may radically change the timeline for a change in ownership. They are things to understand and prepare for ... while hoping they never occur! Consequently, becoming more and more ready for any of these situations can pay huge benefits and protect the owner's wealth.

Here is a quick look at these potential occurrences, the Dismal D's.

Divorce

Divorce is a situation that today arises in nearly half of all families. At best a divorce is distracting. At worst it can be highly disruptive and put a significant financial strain on the business. The stronger the business is when difficulties surface, the more likely they will not result in an untimely sale of the business to resolve the family split.

Disability

We all expect to remain healthy. And most of us do! But, an owner can become disabled from an accident or another life event. Depending on the situation, a disability can be costly. The disability may preclude the owner from continuing to manage the business. If there are good systems and trained managers in the business to maintain operations, there is less probability financial difficulties will transpire.

Death

Just as with a disability, we all hope and expect to live a long life and see the fulfillment of many personal and business goals. Unfortunately, for some owners this will not be the case. An untimely demise of an owner can put untold stress on the family and the business and can precipitate the need for the sale of the business ... often at an inopportune time in the business cycle.

Business Distress

A small business can experience financial hardship from the loss of a key customer, a critical vendor, or an important manager. There are no guarantees that today's success will continue without an interruption or something worse. In the most difficult cases, such problems, especially if coupled with an industry downturn, may require consideration of a transfer to a new owner who has added financial resources to weather the storm.

Lessening the Impact of the Dismal D's

To the extent that a well-prepared business valuation can foster better planning and improve operations, it can lessen the potential impact from the Dismal D's! If a business owner can address the needed changes to make the business more profitable and more transferrable, any loss in value should be mitigated in an untimely sale. The key is to have the business become more and more <u>ready for an unexpected ownership transfer</u> as part of the annual operational business planning.

> ## "Readiness" for a *planned* or an *unplanned* ownership change is a critical attribute of continuous importance!

This is IMPORTANT! The secret is that doing the things such as developing and executing effective strategic and business plans to improve near-term operational outcomes are, in the main, <u>the same things that enhance transferability</u>. Consequently, the task of every business owner is to use all the information found in a business valuation, along with other tools and techniques that are available, to strengthen their business on a consistent basis.

With this background on the history and use of some new knowledge it is time to add a little to the understanding of what "value" is and is not. That is the topic of the next chapter which should decidedly improve the quality of your interactions with your key professionals, your A Team of appraisers, accountants, and attorneys.

An additional thought for consideration: Reaching the value and operational potential that lies within your business is in your hands as *you write that story with improved knowledge to plan and take management actions.* The advantages you can realize from reading and studying this book can make a notable difference in the coming chapters of your "business story." That is where the "REAL VALUE" becomes personally available to you ... in any business valuation!

The "real value," to you, comes from the benefits you can create as you write the future chapters of your business story. The resulting increase in business value and improved "ease of transfer" is the "real gain" for you and your family.

CHAPTER 02 | VALUE DEFINITIONS

LET'S TAKE A close look at what the business valuator, an appraiser, is saying with the statement of purpose for the valuation. It says the valuation is seeking a "fair market value" estimate for your business as of a certain date. To understand more about how this is done we need to define some terms that you may have heard used or misused over the years.

Almost everyone has heard the term "fair market value" and in general believe this is what everyone is always talking about. That glancing understanding of a value measure and/or definition is not always true. It is an important reference point in a valuation discussion. But it should be properly defined and put in proper perspective as to its origin and use.

There are THREE primary definitions of value used by valuation analysts and two other definitions that are important to understand. Let's review them. We will do that and make some notes on an additional definition now in vogue in the valuation community. The short diversion into these definitions will provide direct edification and become useful as a future reference. Let's start with the one that we all think we know from the various discussion we have had or heard over the years.

Fair Market Value

Fair Market Value (FMV) has a statutory definition. What does that really mean? Well ... it is a <u>value defined by law</u> that is used in specific legal proceeding. In practice, this term is used in and misused in many other contexts.

The definition of Fair Market Value is based on a hypothetical scenario that is critical to comprehend. It is an ESTIMATE of VALUE based on a group of attributes for a given situation. This value measure is just that: an estimate based on analysis. It is, in fact, as you may have heard "quickly explained" at different times based on the willing-buyer-willing-seller standard.

Let's take a step beyond what we have heard and pieced together in our minds and look at the formal definition.

Fair market value is considered to represent the value at which a willing seller and a willing buyer, both being informed of the relevant facts about the business, could reasonably conduct a transaction, neither party acting under any compulsion to do so. Court decisions frequently state that the hypothetical buyer and seller are assumed to be able, as well as willing, to trade and to be well informed about the property and the market for such property.

If you look up the definition on the internet it may go on to state this: *An estimate of fair market value may be developed either on precedent or extrapolation. Since market transactions are often not observable for assets such as privately held businesses versus most personal and real property,* FMV must be estimated.

An estimate of fair market value is, therefore, subjective due to the circumstances of place, time, the existence of comparable precedents, and the evaluation principles involved. Opinions on value are always based upon subjective interpretation (and analysis) of available information at the time of assessment.

This is the legal "value definition" referenced in estate filing, shareholder disputes, and in most divorce proceeding. *(Some state statutes may specify a slightly different definition for divorce or dissident shareholder actions.)*

Most importantly, this is the value we often use in discussions unless some other definition is specified. Business valuations prepared for use in planning seek to establish the "fair market value" for the business's equity. That is the ownership interest for the business entity.

The function and purpose of valuations (appraisals), unless otherwise stated, is to develop an opinion for the "Fair Market Value" (FMV) of the subject business. This is the "baseline" value sought. This "value estimate" may be different from the actual value realized in a transaction, which has a different value definition. That noted, the transaction result for many, many businesses may be very close to, or well within a range of value estimated in a properly researched and developed valuation report.

Liquidation Value

Liquidation value, which is not always shown in a business appraisal, is another estimated value based on appropriate analysis. (For appraisals, when included, this liquidation value is normally estimated for "an orderly liquidation.") The value estimate provides <u>insight into the downside risk associated with a group of assets</u>, such as an operating business. Liquidation value is important to you, the business owner, because it is also useful in assessing commercial lending limits for deal structuring.

The detailed definition of "Liquidation Value" is this: Liquidation value (LV) is the total worth of a company's physical assets if it were to go out of business and the assets sold. The liquidation value is the value of company real estate, fixtures, equipment, and inventory. Intangible assets are normally excluded from a company's liquidation value.

Both "Fair Market Value" and "Liquidation Value" are measures *(knowledgeable estimates)* of value with importance in planning and an understanding of potential deal structures. The precise uses of both of these value points will be addressed in later chapters to show specifically how they can yield some important information to augment the business owner's prospective "someday" deal picture. *(You can use these tools to optimally structure "your deal" when the time is right!)*

Investment Value

In transaction discussions we also hear quite frequently about "Investment Value" (IV) Investment value is typically discussed as if it was a higher value than FMV. That is not a correct definition of investment value. Nor is it always or even mostly true that investment value is a "higher value."

The operative definition of the "Investment Value" for an operating business is this: **Investment value** *is the* **value** *of a property to a particular investor. When applied to a business it is the direct result of an actual transaction between two active parties ... the specific buyer and the specific seller.*

Let's reduce that definition to a single sentence for reference since it is so often misused and misunderstood. Investment value is the value of a transaction between a specific buyer and a specific seller. If there's synergy—in other words, if there are benefits beyond a financial standalone purchase for the buyer—there may be a final deal at a price above FMV. Similarly, if the strength of one of the participants *(buyer or seller)* is greater than the other it can affect final pricing. Investment value may be higher *or* lower than FMV in specific cases.

However, investment value, for most transactions, is very, very close to fair market value. For the investor *(a business acquirer)* in a specific subject business to pay significantly more for a business, the acquirer would have to see uses for the assets held by the selling business that could yield a much higher return (or profit) within the combined entities. It is this motivation, based on other ownership and the related knowledge, that can increase the value achieved in a specific transaction.

Ownership benefits that were not achieved as a standalone business entity can change the buyer's value assessment. How you, as a business owner, should and can assess such potential is a subject for direct discussion with your personal transaction advisor ... when that process begins.

The best investment bankers will always be seeking to establish any potential benefits within a specific deal to increase the price realized by the seller. However, this is an analysis that is not directly developed within a valuation since the "buyer" is a hypothetical financial buyer and not a specific purchaser whose key business attributes and potential uses of the acquired business's assets can be analyzed.

 Here is a summary that provides a quick reference for the values defined to this point and their primary reference use. What is important to remember is that the job of a business owner is to understand what creates value and then improve the attributes of the business that can drive that value.

Here is a summary of the utility of the primary values as defined:

Different DEFINITIONS of *VALUE*

- *Fair Market Value – Hypothetical (Rev. 59-60)*
- *Liquidation Value – Downside Risk Measure*
- *Investment Value – Specific Deal Participants*

Enterprise Value

Numerous business-oriented television shows often reference "Enterprise Value" (EV) when discussing publicly traded stocks. This is also a term that is used more and more today to bridge the communications gap by expanding the understanding or misunderstanding of what "invested capital" really is within a business valuation (appraisal) environment.

The definition of "Enterprise Value" is this: Enterprise Value or EV is a measure of a company's worth. As a measure of company worth, it is superior to other measures such as just Equity Market Capitalization, and it also includes the Market Value of Debt. Enterprise Value is often termed as the takeover price because, in the event of a takeover, EV is the selling price of the company ... debt free.

The important takeaway is that the equity of a business, the objective in a Fair Market Value (FMV) business valuation assignment, can be computed by determining the Enterprise Value and deducting the company's interest-bearing debt. A further discussion of this term and value measure will be addressed in the section in chapter 5 defining the development and use of "Invested Capital," which has a direct connection in practice.

This is IMPORTANT! In that *Invested Capital* is defined as a business's interesting bearing debt plus the business's equity, *(the total capital deployed in the business)*, there is a technical difference on the exclusion of "cash" on the balance sheet when applying Enterprise Value to publicly traded stocks. If, in the valuation process, the working capital is "right sized," then this additional definition can be used to discuss the <u>value of a company on a debt-free basis</u>.

Other Values Measures

Some states have developed a **"FairValue"** statutory definition of value for application to shareholder disputes and divorce actions. If someone uses this term, you should seek specific definition for the jurisdiction you are in. These statues are usually based on FMV in some manner.

Other definitions for specific purposes such as Buy-Sell Agreements are used. Once such term is **"Agreed-Upon Value"** to signfy that the parties have periodically agreed on a specific value, for a certain period of time, and/or a method to update that value. Such values and their driving defintion, based on valuation principles, should be clearly laid out and understood. It is essential this is done in order to reach an agreement.

Emotional Value

As a business owner, you don't want to let the emotional attachments you feel take over your thinking. When this happens, you could miss key opportunities. You want to be prepared and avoid regrets. After years of work and the development of many important relationships, it can be most difficult to part with your business and to change your personal "identity."

Too often the parts of your business you will miss most can override solid assessment of offers in hand. That is the reason that it is important to not only prepare your business for a transaction with the information assembled from a business valuation, but also to prepare yourself for this change of daily activity and your "position in the community."

Owners, at times, hold out for a higher-than-justified value on their business to keep from addressing some underlying transition issues. Often such hesitance to act is rooted in the emotional value they attach to the business and how their identity, in his or her mind, might be impacted by completing the sale. One of the benefits you should realize from this book is to better assess the "value" of your business and to view your other feelings in their proper perspective. The more you know and understand about "business value," the better prepared you will be for that day when it will be the right time to make this decision.

There is a place to look for more insight and information on preparing yourself in this environment. It is Chapter 5, "The Hardest Part of the Answer" in the internationally bestselling book: *When Is the Right Time to Sell My Business?* This chapter provides some important information for every business owner. Use it to prepare yourself for the biggest business deal of your business lifetime. *(The book is available on Amazon in Kindle, Paperback, and Audio versions.)*

Deductions from personal observations over decades of investment banking practice emphasize over and over the importance of this broader preparation for a sale ... even if that sale is far into the future. The key word really is **READINESS!** Your Readiness! Be ready by assessing current postures and continuing improvement day after day.

Let's review. It should be remembered that "fair market value" (FMV) is based on an IRS ruling from 1959. Rev 59-60 is summarized in Appendix A. It provides an easy reference for personal edification. It is a hypothetical value estimate, whereas "investment value" is based on actual deal results between specific buyer and seller and their relative strengths and motivations. *(As noted, experienced investment bankers will work hard to discover if there is a material difference between FMV and IV for a specific buyer or group of buyers.)*

Liquidation value is a solid point of reference that provides a good indication of the upper lending limit for commercial bank lending. *This is a very, very important limit to know when negotiating a transfer of ownership in a business.* Why? Because it may immediately indicate the need to consider "seller financing" to achieve an optimal price in a future transaction.

A business owner's knowledge and facility in using these value measures in analyzing their business will permit the uncovering of important features of the business and previewing potential deal structures. There is a graphic in chapter 5 along with a referenced example to provide further edification on definitions and terms within the valuation arena.

CHAPTER 03

RESEARCH YIELDS BENEFITS

A BUSINESS VALUATION is a major research project. It involves a detailed look at the general economy and how it impacts the business. Even a midsize business is a very small ship on a big ocean. Economic storms like ocean currents can cause them to get off course … or worse. Area economics play a great role in the development of a business.

A business valuation looks extensively at the local economy as well. Part of this research addresses the difficulties of attracting and retaining skilled employees. Knowing how certain industry segments operate is critically important to sustain growth, which is a key driver of value. As the owner, you will want to take some extra time to see and reflect on what the appraiser uncovers via research. There may be something to consider and change in hiring or other operational or marketing actions.

Industry analysis also involves assessment of inputs to strategies to optimize revenue growth and performance. Information on the subject business's strengths and weaknesses are very important to planning. *This is the traditional SWOT analysis*—strengths, weaknesses, opportunities, and threats—*that is part of all good strategic planning processes.* A valuation will provide those insights and give an independent look at the individual business from this perspective. Clarifying where the business is in the larger economic picture helps determine future performance projections.

The general economic and regulatory environment and specific environmental legislation impact future performance differently in various industry sectors. Capital markets affect investment plans and change over time. The alternatives for investors are dependent on all these factors. As a business owner you want to always be thinking about how these external dynamics can affect your business. A valuation should provide you with an updated list of considerations in this area to monitor. *You do not want to get blindsided by a pending regulatory change in the middle of a major expansion or transaction.*

The business valuation takes a deeper look into the business, its management, its marketing techniques, its strategies, its business systems, and its financial factors. These assessments provide risk measurements in each area.

A reference of the initial information analyzed in the Business Valuation Process is provided in Appendix B for reference. This list should provide some beginning understanding on what internal information will be analyzed as part of the first phase of the valuation process.

This is IMPORTANT! The benefits of measuring and managing business value cannot be overstated! An owner's work in this area is the foundation to the preparation for a successful transaction when the time is right! A business valuation involves in-depth analysis in six fundamental areas:

- *Macroeconomic Factors*
- *Industrial Factors*
- *Business Operating Factors*
- *Capital Market Factors*
- *Governmental Factors*
- *Financial Factors*

This information within the report should be exercised to the maximum amount required to yield actionable steps to improve cash flows and reduce the risks that prospective buyers may perceive. *The projection of future cash flows should specifically quantify the benefits of ownership ... and give sufficient feedback to prompt changes when indicated.*

The business valuation process is summarized in the following graphic. It shows the six different factors that affect the business and business value. Some are directly in the control of the owner. Others are not! The challenge is to become aware of the influence of each to be able to adapt to the changes that will inevitably arrive.

Business Valuation Analysis

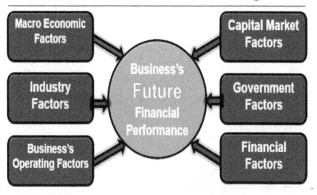

This is IMPORTANT! Macroeconomics addressed within the report should be studied to have a solid understanding of the larger operating environment and the implication for the subject company *(Your Company)*. The numerous factors within the company's primary and secondary industry segments will directly impact operating potential. *(Buyers are searching for businesses within growing industries with solid statistical profiles.)* This area requires insightful analysis to assess and amend strategies and projected results. Similarly, the business's characteristics that distinguish it from its competitors must be understood. *(When you use this information to reposition your company's target markets—even a little—it could have a meaningful impact on the value of your business.)*

**"WHAT'S HAPPENING? OUR BUSINESS USED
TO BE AT THE HEAD OF THE PACK!
WE DOMINATED THE MARKET!"**

The external factors from the capital markets and government laws and regulations that control the operating environment and the way the valuation analyst assesses them should be fully comprehended. *(All of this information is an input to your planning and review processes.)* Prospective changes in this area should be included in the projections of future performance. The financial results for the company and its competitors are essential to determine the use of resources and effectiveness of management.

All six groups of factors will directly and indirectly control future cash flows and company value. The valuator must integrate their relative relationships into all phases of the valuation project. Part of what makes a good report is that it provides the reader (the business owner) with the ability to replicate the valuation process in different time frames.

What can be learned from this portion of a business valuation? How can you put the knowledge to good use. For example, the typical SWOT analysis shows where actions can have the greatest benefit. This and other information can be used to develop new strategies or to exercise existing business strategies! Optimization and improvement comes from execution of the right strategies. Growth prospects and growth drivers should be evident from a valuation.

It should be remembered that SWOT and other such business intelligence are only beneficial if they generate strategic plans that can be followed by actionable tactics. It is ultimately plans and actions at the project level that deliver meaningful results.

The valuation processes used by professional buyers show clearly how they are going to view your business. Measuring and managing value long before contemplating a transaction makes significant differences. Sometime value increases of two times to five times or more are clearly possible.

Let's take a look at what can be done: One of my early clients was struggling with low margins and slow growth. Once he had the valuation in hand and could see the places to add revenue and the benefit of margin improvement he set out on a major set of new actions. Three years later, his business had revenues growth of just over 20 percent. But, in this same time frame, the company's gross margins had increased by over 4 percent and the overhead was reduced by just under 2 percent of sales. This improved metrics more than doubled the value of his business in that three-year period with modest growth. Plus, this owner now had a lot more cash flow each year to use in the business or to "take home to his family"!

The comparative financial position of the business within the industry is important. <u>Buyers are looking for businesses in the top quartile of any industry</u>. You want to use the information in the valuation to move from wherever you are ... to the top of your industry! You want to use the information to secure your competitive position. This focus helps to address customer diversification, develop management, enhance market position, and improve the overall performance of the business.

What is meant by "financial position"? On the income statement side, if you look at the profile sheet from most Private Equity Groups (PEGs) you will see that they are looking for businesses with earnings before interest and taxes (EBIT) greater than 15 percent. These professional investors also want to see <u>company growth greater than the industry</u> in which the business operates.

On the balance sheet, there are a number of measures that the valuator will do to show the subject business versus the industry. A buyer will want to recognize, for example, why the working capital levels are higher or lower than competitors. But, they may also see opportunity here to free some cash post-closing.

As the owner, you want to understand the implication and the company's position in some detail so you can make changes over time to move into the top quartile among your top industry competitors.

A valuation report will show how to reduce risk and to increase performance *(the reward of ownership)* to affect the most probable future transaction price. The tools and techniques can be put directly to good use.

Once you have a current value for your business and can begin to see where you might take it in the next five to ten years, <u>your personal financial planning gaps should become clear and relatively easy to measure</u>. This is the difference between the future needs, you and your financial advisor project, and the cash the business will provide. This is one of the reasons that your estate attorney as well as your personal financial advisor can make direct use of the combination of data points in a valuation report.

"You still believe we don't need
NO STINKING PLAN?!"

The projected taxes to be paid in a future sale will help you determine the net projected proceeds from a transfer of ownership. In the simple example of a company review, we are going to present the tools and data used to make these computations. This should help clarify the look into this area sufficient for you to be able to ask the questions when you read your report. *(Net cash from a transaction is different than the price for the assets transferred! It is the "net cash" that will be part of your overall personal asset based eventually used to support your future lifestyle.)*

By combining the information in the historic balance sheet and the "tangible assets" interim value estimate, <u>an excellent estimate of both</u> <u>"recapture" and "capital gains" taxes can be developed</u>. Please take a close look at the example business valuation information to see exactly how to make these calculations.

Always Remember: It is not the specific price achieved that matters. *It is the amount of money you will have after taxes that makes the* *difference to you and your family.*

The information in the valuation report helps you set new goals if required. That should be done early enough to take actions to reach the goal. Managing value takes time and effort. The better knowledge you have about what you can and should do, and the earlier you put it to use, the better outcomes you are going to get.

Measuring Operations

Measuring the results of business operations prompts timely enhancement of plans ... and actions! Study after study shows that measured activities achieve a 20 percent or more greater output. This is equally true at the entity valuation level as well. So, measure value, improve operating results *(the benefits of ownership)* and move that value toward your goal.

© Michael H. Marks

"Sorry grasshopper, I do not have a vision of the value of your business. My advice is to go out and seek a professional!"

Chris Mercer, one of the leaders in the business appraisal industry for decades, makes the point that most people pay up to 1 percent or more in annual fees for the management of the publicly traded stocks and bonds they own. *(Wealth management fees do drop to < 0.50 percent on accounts with asset values > $5M)*. Chris's point is that every business owner should see the prudence and benefits of allocating some funds toward annual or bi-annual business valuations to provide management information for the larger part of most business owner's total wealth. (Often > 80 percent) For further insights into the points that Chris so effectively makes, please refer to

The One Percent Solution ... by Chris Mercer

As noted, there are fantastic paybacks and a long-term impact of consistently measuring and managing business value. That fact cannot be overstated! An owner's work in this area is the foundation to the preparation for a successful transaction <u>when the time is right</u>! But equally important are the near-term operational benefits that can be realized by adjustments of plans and actions based on the information presented in a valuation report. To achieve optimal results a simple feedback systems should be deployed and religiously used to plan and re-plan as shown in the following chart:

Managing Business Value

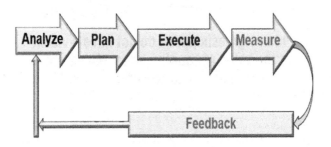

To gain some added benefit from the valuation report, look for measurements noted or other elements that you can use to monitor your ongoing business. (Deploy this basic system model ... and you will be amazed at the improvement you will achieve over time.) In summary, here is what can be learned directly from the analysis of the economy, industry and the business in each business valuation report:

- *Strengths and Weakness of Operations*
- *Growth Prospect for the Market and Business*
- *Comparative Position within Your Industry*
- *Value Drivers Identified to Enhance Opportunities*

In some reports, the analyst may use the Five Forces Framework model developed by Michael Porter. An analysis of the five forces effecting competition provides and in-depth look at the industry and/or market segments. The forces are:

- *Bargaining Power of Suppliers*
- *Bargaining Power of Buyers*
- *Threat of Substitutes*
- *Threat of New Entrants*
- *Industry Rivalry*

In other reports, this information may be provided in a more indirect manner. It is important to take a few minutes to appreciate these competitive forces and how they have and will influence business results. Effective use of the intelligence acquired will pay direct benefits in the business operation and in an eventual transaction. Every professional acquirer of privately held business will perform this competitive analysis as an early hurdle in their acquisition process.

This is IMPORTANT! The valuation analyst and the business owners should uncover and discuss a number of business and deal elements. The research and industry sections for the report should be the basis for these discussions. *(Information on the optimal approach to such interactive discussions will be addressed in the succeeding chapters within the example shown for reference.)* If there is something you do not fully understand in the report or how the valuation analyst assessed the force of these factors ... ASK! These include but should not be limited to these business areas:

- *Risk Contributors and Mitigation Strategies*
- *Management Development (Succession)*
- *Most Probable Transaction Price "Today" ... and in the "future" for use in estate planning*

- *Most Probable Deal Structure*
- *Allocation of Assets in a Projected Transaction*
- *Projected Taxes on a Transaction (Before Optimization)*

Different parts of this information can be directly used in development of personal financial plans and in estate plans and for use in annual business operational planning. This is how you create some REAL VALUE with clear-eyed actions!

Let's take a little closer look into the external and internal sources of information used today in all business analysis.

External Info Sources

The good news for every business owner is that the cost and availability of external information has radically improved over the last three decades. Just thirty years ago, the research information used in analysis and found in most valuation reports could have cost in excess of $50,000. Today, the costs are less than 10 percent of that level. Business valuation professionals have access to and will find many different sources of information for use in reports to help them with their analysis of the "subject company" relative to the peers and leaders in an industry or industry segment.

This is IMPORTANT! Today there are a large number of resources that are available to valuation analyst, investment bankers, and business owners. Please ask the appraisal analyst for the list of information sources, if they do not show directly in the report which sources were accessed and, if it makes sense, ask for a copy of the raw report for an additional personal review. *Depending on the source and type of licensed use, the valuator may not be able to provide the full background report. But, in most cases, there may be few such difficult restrictions.*

<u>Trade organization</u> have proven to be excellent sources of information that may not be publicly available. If you are not a member of the different trade groups in your industry, it may be time to consider adding them to your mix of sources for inputs to planning and value creation.

Internal Info Sources

Every company develops and produces internal reports for management in different ways. Regardless of what terms or titles these reports take, the following information should be available for the valuation analyst as well as the business owner. The valuation analyst may look at the reported information in several different ways to enhance understanding of the business. Here is the beginning list of information sources or groupings of data:

- *General Market Research (product specific)*
- *Target Market Research (new and future)*
- *Marketing Methods and Results*
- *Pricing Practices and Margin Growth (or decline)*
- *Distribution Channels/Strategies/Contributions*
- *Work Force (trained and available)*
- *Critical Management (in place and for succession planning)*
- *Facilities/Equipment (Economic depreciation and CAP-X requirements to support plans)*

In addition to these areas, both the valuation analyst and the business owners should identify these additional company attributes:

- *Marketing and Sales Systems (or lack thereof)*
- *Product and Deliver Systems (or lack thereof)*
- *Financial Control Systems (or lack thereof)*
- *Operating Measurement Systems (or lack thereof)*

Your company's financial reporting process (system) may require some improvement to make it a better management tool. The periodic nature of a tightly crafted internal financial reporting system can have value in itself that cannot be overemphasized. Don't hesitate to use your new knowledge and your accounting advisor's expertise to make any indicated adjustments.

Beyond these systems, some deeper research into the financial condition of the business, both current and under different future scenarios, either will show clearly in the report or can be usually be made available from the valuator's work papers.

Don't kid yourself. If you need to tighten up your business systems ... do it! *(Systems Sell!)*

A term that you may see used in the report is "leverage," both regarding the balance sheet position and the analysis of the income statement.

The valuator, as he or she replicates the buying process, will look closely at historic debt level and gross margin company trends versus the industry as discussed earlier. Part of this analysis will be the establishment of a breakeven point for current overhead in place. *(This exact information may not show in the report so ask the analyst for their assessment to compare to what you, as the business owner, have developed.)*

This is IMPORTANT! In the balance sheet analysis, as seen through the recasting process, the assets that will be retained and those ultimately offered for sale should be separated. All of the assets required to continue ongoing successful business operations will be part of the "assets to be sold." Other assets will be separated and retained for personal use or independent disposal. The following graphic provides a beginning look at the type of asset that would be separated and retained by the owner.

This graphic only shows the different assets by class to advance this specific point for the need to separate assets into a group that will be retained versus those that are an integral part of the operations and will be transferred. Any refining adjustment in the proper level of cash within the working capital analysis is an isolated separate activity.

This discussion may prompt you to take your first look at what assets should be part of a transaction and what assets should be retained. First take some extra time to place all the assets that are anything to do with your business into these two groups. Over time you may want to prudently reduce the assets that are not required to operate the business ... to develop a clear picture of the assets that are integral to the business operation.

Current Assets

Cash & Equivalents
Accounts Receivable
Inventory
Other Current Assets

Fixed Assets

Land
Buildings & Improvements
Equipment
Vehicles

Other Assets

Officers' Life Insurance
Marketable Securities
Organizational Costs

All Assets are Stated in
Accordance with:

Accounting Standards

If the real estate assets are owned by the business, they can be leased to a new owner and consequently should be addressed separated by the valuator. The lease should replace any expenses associates with the direct ownership of such real estate with a **"fair market lease rate"** (rent) in the analysis.

Real estate normally carries different rates of return than an operating business due to the perceived differences in risk. This is also an important reason for separation. The other and more important reason is that astute buyers want to deploy the maximum amount of their cash to generate growth ... not tie it up in real estate.

Other assets such as insurance on the life of the owner and marketable securities would normally be retained by the seller. These are examples of typical assets and other personal or special-use assets (such as camps, condos, airplanes, etc.) that should be removed from the balance sheet as part of the tangible asset analysis. This separation is a first step toward determining, in a hypothetical transaction, what will be transferred and what will be retained.

Non-Balance Sheet Assets

Somewhere in the overall investigation, the analyst will either directly or indirectly assess a number of assets that typically do not show on the balance sheet. They are key assets nonetheless. In some cases a look at these assets may uncover some real value or almost none to the company.

These "other assets" may be major drivers of cash flow for the business. To the extent that they ARE not, they may have little value. So, the fact that they are not directly on the balance sheet does not mean that their presence is not evident within the historic financial statements. At times, these assets may exist but be underutilized and may not be generating the potential related cash flow. Look specifically for any type of "asset" a valuation analyst might uncover; *these are the same assets you should go back and look at in your business to see if there is hidden, potential value in their future use.*

- *Customer Lists*
- *Supplier (Vendor) Lists*
- *Special Licenses*

- *Trade Names*
- *Patents*
- *Research and Development (not yet commercialized)*
- *Contracts (generating recurring revenue)*
- *Proprietary Processes*
- *Systems (software and others)*
- *Experience Ratings (workmen's compensation)*
- *Reputation as an Employer (do not under-estimate)*

This is IMPORTANT! *This last one, Employer's Reputation, may be much more important than most people know! Why would that be the case? Because attracting and retaining the best employees over time will have a major impact on how any business operates!*

© Michael H Marks

"Yippee! It's 8:00 o'clock and we get to start work!"

VALUATION PRINCIPLES & APPROACHES

Valuation Principles

THREE BASIC VALUATION principles are the foundation to all valuation work:

- *Principle of Alternatives*
- *Principle of Substitution*
- *Principle of Future Benefits*

Please bear with this part of the discussion as these principles are addressed. You will see how important these foundational principles are to the overall use and application of knowledge found in valuation reports.

A good appreciation of these three principles will help you assess, compare, and understand not only the opinion of value developed in the business appraisal *but also (someday in the future)* <u>the basis for the different offers from prospective qualified buyers</u>. A facility with these three concepts *(principles)* will permit *you (the business owner)* to increase your awareness of "what the professional business buyers are regularly doing in the market."

The first foundational concept is the **principle of alternatives**. All investors have choices in the market place every day. Any investor can either invest in low-risk investments like treasury bills or high-risk investments like venture capital for early stage companies. Or any investment with a risk profile that is in between. Public equities, debt, and municipal bonds all carry different risk and reward profiles. A small, privately held business is a riskier investment than public stocks and bonds. <u>The valuator will determine and show in the report information to help you fully understand where your business fits on that continuum</u>. It is important to clearly think through how an investor looks at alternatives.

This is IMPORTANT! Think of it this way. Every day you are making an investment decision to reinvest in your own business. You are deciding to "hold onto the investment." So you really want to understand the risks and rewards. By not acting to sell ... you are really rebuying the business today. That is great if it's what you want to be doing with the business investment and it continues to meet your risk and/or reward profile and requirements.

This is IMPORTANT! Second is the **principle of substitution**. Any investor has a variety of opportunities available. They have options between investments with a certain risk and/or reward profile. <u>A buyer can purchase another business in your industry, or a similar type of business in a related industry</u>. Those substitutes may have different characteristics or may better match the investor's objectives. What substitutions investors might consider is important. This knowledge will help you develop and position your business for a transaction.

To have an edge on that day when you finally decide "it is time to sell," you want to stand out from your competitors in the market place. The major attribute that clearly communicates that your business is different and better is the <u>development of a specific competitive advantage</u>.

That advantage may be in product development and design, marketing strength, or in any number of other operational areas.

Let's think about Private Equity Groups (PEGs) as potential acquirers. Each private equity group will have industry preferences for investments due to their knowledge and experience. They will have both alternative (different) industries or industry segments in which they choose to seek investments as well as other specific businesses they identify in each business segment.

These professional investors are reviewing hundreds of companies to find the right one. All of the prospective business investments they consider are "substitutes" to investing in your business.

The third principle normally carries the most weight in transactions after an investment passes the tests presented by the other two principles. It is the **principle of future benefits**. People buy businesses based on what they will deliver for them in the future. This performance yields investment returns and lifestyle cash flow. You want to understand how the valuation analyst quantified and analyzed all anticipated benefits your business can deliver.

Don't pass up the opportunity to question the projection of income the analyst makes in the valuation. Learn how these estimates of future benefits were developed and on what basis the estimates were made. This information will do two things. First, you can see in detail how buyers will approach and make their own projections. And, second you will see what you have done and can do to improve future projections.

This is IMPORTANT! Future benefits drive most business transactions. Such benefits come directly from the earning power of the business. This principle of future benefits is a critical foundation concept.

Oliver Wendell Holmes, one of the great jurists of all time, put this into perspective when he once said:

> ## "All values are based on an anticipation of the future."

Valuation Approaches

Valuation activity and analysis fall within three areas. They are the **Asset Approach, Income Approach**, and the **Market Approach**. Each of these are broad areas of analysis. Within each approach, one or more valuation methods can be applied to develop interim valuation estimates that will be part of your valuation report.

Interim Value Determinations

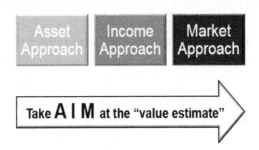

A good analyst is able to assess and iterate what might happen in the marketplace and to opine on the ultimate fair market value of the business. It is the fair market value estimate that you are seeking as a baseline data point for further analysis and planning. The entire business valuation process takes aim at this value estimate. The concepts involved in these three approaches (AIM) and the specific methods applied by valuators are explored in chapters 7 through 9.

Speculation on investment value under different scenarios would be outside the scope of a typical business valuation. Any needed analysis of this type should be completed only after a specific buyer or unique group of buyers, with known business attributes, are present in a deal environment.

The report should permit you, the business owner, to understand sufficiently what was done within the different approaches for you to replicate the process. Specifically, any report reader should be able to reapply, with new input data, the process steps to develop a revised interim valuation estimate.

This is IMPORTANT! No valuation result is exact. The FMV estimate will be in the center of a range of values for your understanding and use. To remind yourself of this fact, you can use that little acronym,

AIM (Assets, Income, and Market), to think of the three different approaches to value analysis applied by professionals. If the valuation estimated developed by the three approaches does not surround a "target area," it is possible that there may be some reason to reassess the results. A number of valuation methods may be employed within each approach as interim estimates are determined. There should be an understandable relationship between the different interim estimates of value.

Let's look at what you might see. Perhaps the tangible assets estimate is significantly higher than the income methods estimate. If this is the case, the analyst has found that the assets in place (after separating out non-operating assets) are not generating an acceptable return. If this is the message, you (the owner) would want to step back and truly understand why the assets were not delivering anticipated benefits of ownership.

What you want to see is the income methods generating an estimate that is greater than the tangible asset estimate. That means you and your team are effectively deploying the assets in the market place and creating some "intangible value." Don't hesitate to investigate the thinking and sources of asset valuation information with the analyst if the different valuation methods diverge to any great degree.

05

THE VALUATION TARGET

THE VALUATION WORLD first seeks the fair market value (FMV) of the business on a debt-free basis. That is the "price discovery" within the valuation (appraisal) process. (That is the "target value" sought within the valuation process.) To develop the FMV estimate for the business entity, all the interim valuation work is applied to the business as if it were debt free. In practice the analyst starts by seeking the value of the entire enterprise debt free (i.e. the "Enterprise Value"). In the valuation environment, the essentially equivalent term "Invested Capital" is used.

This is IMPORTANT! So here is the definition of a term you want to fully understand: It is INVESTED CAPITAL! "Invested Capital" is defined as the shareholders equity plus the interest-bearing debt. It's the price of the total assets of your business that will be transferred in a transaction. You, the owner, would then pay off the existing debt ... and retain any non-operating assets.

A good way to get a solid grip on this financial concept is to look back at the last home you purchased. You bought that house with two financial components that added to the price paid. You assembled your down payment. That was your equity, the amount you put into the home. You arranged a loan and an associated mortgage with your commercial bank or another lending institution for the balance required to pay the agreed price. This portion becomes your personal debt. Combined, the two financial components provide the total price paid for the home.

Example: INVESTED CAPITAL *(for your home)*

Down Payment + Mortgage = Price Paid
(Your EQUITY) + (Your DEBT) = PRICE

Please look at the "home transaction" in summary this way. What you get is the **home!** What you pay is the **down payment <u>plus</u> the loan amount.** The latter is your "total amount paid" to gain ownership of your home *(i.e. your invested capital).*

The same thing is true for a business purchase. The buyer will provide a certain amount of equity and borrow the balance to pay the agreed price for the business. This total capital invested in the business is defined as the "Invested Capital" and it equates directly to the "Price

Paid." Invested capital is the total capital ... a combination of equity and debt. (Shareholders Equity + Interest-bearing Debt).

"Price" = Invested Capital

(Properly adjusted for Working Capital and Other Exclusions)

By this procedure, the analyst will first investigate and estimate the "invested capital" of your business. This is the interim valuation target to identify and understand because it will be the price metric you eventually negotiate for your business assets (the value on a debt-free basis). This value estimate should be properly adjusted for working capital and other exclusions. *(Exclusions are things you're not transferring, like a car or life insurance policy as previously noted.)* Many times the real estate used by the business, as mentioned earlier, may be retained and leased to the new owner. All of these different components to the total assets mix must and should be addressed in the business valuation. The valuation report will provide clarity in these areas.

We noted that Enterprise Value is, with a minor adjustment, another, maybe friendlier and more relatable, term for Invested Capital. The enterprise picture of the business looks like this. It is similar to the home example.

<u>**What you are receiving with a business purchase is**</u>

Working Capital + Fixed Assets + Intangible Assets

<u>**What you are paying is the combination of your**</u>

Equity + Interest-bearing Debt

Let's take a look at a simple graphic to show what occurs in a transaction. The buyer receives the assets of the enterprise in the three distinct asset groups as noted. And the buyer pays the price for the acquired entity (the Enterprise) with a combination of debt and equity.

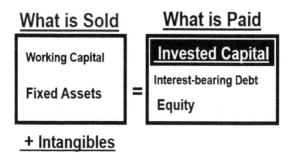

If the three valuation approaches of AIM do not correlate, it may have to do with the exclusions. That is the one place to look to reconcile such differences. Be sure that all three approaches are estimating the "value of the exact same three groups of assets." (These are different "shots" at the same target!)

For example: the income approach estimated the value of the earning power of the business. To operate and deliver this value, the business would require an "adequate amount of working capital." Therefore, the tangible asset method should reflect that same amount of working capital, based on sufficient analysis. *(Any excess or deficiency in working capital should be addressed outside the interim value estimates, that is, in the final determination of value for the subject business.)*

Conversely, in certain situations, since the tangible asset method does not include a value estimate for "intangibles," if these non-balance sheet assets generate a notable amount of cash flow, the two value estimates may be different ... in an understandable and very positive manner.

Your "take away" here is that the "price," as normally discussed for your business, is the value of the business's "invested capital." Since most transaction are "asset sales" not "stock sales," you can see the direct connection in a deal situation.

Accounting Versus Valuation

CHAPTER

06

ECONOMIC FINANCIAL STATEMENTS

EVERY BUSINESS OWNER looks at the monthly and annual financial statements prepared by the company's accountants. These reports are "good enough" to use to manage the business and file tax returns, so why aren't they used directly as the basis for valuation analysis? That is, why is it important to adjust the historic financial statements to "economic" financial statements in preparation for all the valuation report analysis?

It really is pretty simple. Accounting statements are based on "rules" and "tax requirements," and are not designed to reflect market prices and forces. A good way to look at the differences, as well as the complementary elements, between accounting statements and recast "economic" statements is shown in the graphic:

Accounting Versus Appraising

<u>ACCOUNTING</u>

- Largely tax-oriented
- Historical

<u>APPRAISING</u>

Market value-oriented

Based on <u>forecasts</u>

Accounting statements are "a look back" at what has been accomplished. Appraisers use this historic record as a basis to "look forward" (i.e. to forecast the company's future story).

Given that every analyst must have a clear picture of the market value of the company's assets and a full understanding of the earning power, it is critical to develop an "economic" balance sheet and an "economic" income statement. Both parts of the financial statement must fully reflect actual operating market results.

Consequently, a crucial skill for a valuator is the development of "economic financial statements." This skill is required because accounting statements are tax-oriented and do not reflect the economic activity or the current market value of company assets.

The process may seem to be a great mystery. It does not need to be that way. However, it does take some experience and solid analytical skills to effectively develop this important interim picture of the business to set the stage for the valuation process.

There should be NO MYSTERY in how the "recasting process" takes place.

Developing an Economic Financial Statement

It is important to remember that balance sheets provide information on assets and liabilities of the business at a "point in time." And that income statements provide company profit and loss information for a "period of time." Both parts of the financial statement are critical to assessment of any business, especially within a valuation process. Consequently, an analyst will take great care to develop a clear "economic picture" of the business within the recasting adjustment steps.

To deliver this "economic picture" for use, the valuation professional will make adjustments in the following manner.

Balance Sheets

There are two steps required for recasting the balance sheets for your business. They are simple to enumerate but each step must be accomplished in a highly effective manner.

- *Review items line-by-line and adjust their value to market value*
- *Remove all non-operating assets or liabilities*

Income Statement

There are two steps required for recasting the income statement for your business. The analyst's experience and judgment play a larger role in this area.

- *Review each item line-by-line, and adjust each one to market value*
- *Removal of all non-recurring or unique expenses that are not contributing to ongoing operations*

If some assets are valued separately from the operating business entity, any income or expenses associated with those assets should also be separated in the "economic income statement" analysis. *(This is an important adjustment crossover to check for the agreement of the interaction within the financial statement accounts.)*

Typical Income Statement Adjustments

As the analyst proceeds. there are a number of expenses that will require review and testing to see if they are at "market value."

Some of these expenses typically are as follows:

- *Owners' Salary and Benefits*
- *Depreciation and Amortization*
- *Capital Expenditures*
- *Bad Debts*
- *Rental and Lease Expenses*
- *Interest Expense on Debt*
- *Travel Expenses*
- *Vehicle Expenses*
- *Non-Operating Expenses*

An example of an entry in this analysis is an owners' salary and benefits, which often require adjustment to reflect the "total costs" of hiring a manager with equivalent experience and expertise. These adjustment to an "economic" expense on the income statement could be in either direction. The owner's salary may be above or below what the analyst believes to be the appropriate compensation for a theoretical replacement. In both cases, such adjustments would be made to move the historic income statement toward a fully economic income statement.

Similar balance sheet adjustments are made to reflect "market values" in the revised statement.

Typical Balance Sheet Adjustments

- *Accounts Receivable (bad debts)*
- *Inventory ("stale" or "undervalued")*
- *"Cash" (normal working capital level)*
- *Fixed Assets (adjust to replacement value)*
- *Debt (picture of invested capital)*
- *Remove Non-Operating Assets*

One thing you will want to look for in the adjustments of the income statement and balance sheet is that they must coordinate. For example, if there is identification of the need to adjust the value of the inventory, there should be a corresponding adjustment in the material costs within the "costs of goods sold." When you are reviewing your valuation report" or any valuation report, look closely at this interaction within the financial statements.

Let's take a closer look at some of the various types of "normalizing" adjustments to take the tax-oriented company financial statement to an "economic" financial statement position.

*Always remember that you (or an analyst) are working to develop a crystal-clear look at the required **"operating assets"** that must be transferred to permit future operation of the business.*

Non-Operating Assets

This is IMPORTANT! These are any assets that the owner may have accumulated during the ownership period that are <u>not required</u> for daily business functions to produce and deliver goods and services. It may seem as if we are making too much of the issue. It is a big step in a valuation to separate the assets into two groups: those used in the business and those that are not. This focus is here to sensitize you, the business owner, to the fact that a new owner will want only the operating assets and that is what is being valued in the report preparation assignment.

Let's look at what valuators often find in a privately held business that has been built over many years and reflects the owner's interest in a number of ways. A typical example might be an exotic vehicle, an original painting, a *camp (used for meetings and entertaining)*, boats, airplanes, and similar assets. The current owner may have used these assets creatively to help generate revenue and to enhance relationships with key customers, but the new owner will not require or expect to use them to continue running the business. All of these assets should be identified and excluded from the business. *(The value they represent will be added back at the appropriate time to compute the final business value equity estimate, within a corporate or equivalent ownership structure, as of a given date.)*

Excess Financial Assets

Many owners will retain excess cash within the business and make investments in publicly traded stocks or bonds. Unless there is immediate, pressing operational investment use for these assets, they are clearly not part of the "going concern." They would be retained by the selling owner. Consequently, the appraiser will identify these financial assets and separate them from the balance sheet for proper inclusion in the value summary. *(You, the business owner, still own them all; they are just not part of the operating business for which the interim value is being estimated.)*

Cash value in life insurance policies fall into this same area unless those policies would be transferred to the new owner. Since the acquirer will develop their own capital structure, it is very unlikely that there would be any "business use for such personal life insurance assets." *(An analysis of the best future use for life insurance asset should be the subject of a separate analysis by the appropriate advisors.)*

Real Estate

In addition to real estate assets, such as a camp, the real estate used directly in the business may often be retained by the current owner. Such real estate should be valued independently and a "fair market lease rate" developed for both the edification of the owner and for direct use in the income statement analysis within the report investigations.

If the business real estate is retained, the owner will have to address and manage or sell this valued asset to manage or sell as a separate set of actions going forward. This may be an important input into both retirement and estate planning. Additionally, if the real estate is leased to the new owner, the annual payments will become a measurable component in the owner's future personal cash flow.

Excess (Or Insufficient) Working Capital

One of the most important segments of the total internal business analysis by the valuator will be to establish the required level of "working capital" for the business. This analysis will be based on both industry medians and the specific operating characteristic of the subject business. A "cash conversion cycle" analysis may be employed by the analyst to make a final determination for the needed amount of working capital to support and carry out business functions.

This "required level" of working capital can then be compared to the actual working capital resident in the business, as of the valuation date. Any difference between the two measurements will become either "excess" or "insufficient" working capital. If there is excess working capital, that amount should be segmented and added back to the interim value estimates. Conversely, any deficit in working capital would be deducted from such interim estimates.

This is IMPORTANT! This working capital analysis within the valuation report should be studied by the owner. It will become a point of negotiation in any future transaction. The buyer will assert that high levels of working capital should be included as an integrated part of the business. Consequently, solid understanding of this key "current assets and liability" assessment will permit better and more effective negotiating results. Plus, this new knowledge should be of immediate use in determining how to best use these liquid assets in the business or if prudent, to put them in your personal hands.

Exhibit 1 in the Exhibits section at the back of the book provides a graphic layout for assembly of the various components in a potential transaction. *(This exhibit will be referred to at different places in this book and will ultimately serve as a way to summarize some of what is learned and can be learned from a business valuation.)*

By entering the separate value estimates for each identifiable portion of your business, you can see both "how they add up" and "what you should or should not include" in the assets offered for sale. This chart is one of the important tools available for you to begin to understand that the total value estimate for your business, as it is today, is much more than "a single number"!

All of this important "recasting" work leads to results that are an essential part of the professional efforts in all business appraisals and in business brokerage. The better the work, the more solid the foundation of the valuation and/or the reference basis for use in planning an ultimate transaction.

This is IMPORTANT! In summary, the recasting work to develop an "economic" financial statement results in the underpinnings for the succeeding application of valuation methods. This analysis is also going to be the basis for the negotiation discussions in any future transaction environment.

The "recast result" for the income statement is to

- *Develop a basis for analysis of company history*
- *Provide a basis for future earnings projections*

The "recast result" for the balance sheet is to

- *Separate non-operating or excess assets for separate consideration*
- *Develop an <u>estimate of the market value of the tangible assets</u> deployed in the business*

"We were doing great, but then
sales just started falling. I'm
not sure what happened!"

Don't let technology or other changes
impact the future value of your business.
Assess management's ability to adapt.

CHAPTER 07

PART 1: ASSET VALUATION ANALYSIS

As SUGGESTED PREVIOUSLY, all buyers will be looking for the earning power as well as the market value of business assets as a basis for both pricing and financing. Never overlook the fact that accounting is always tax-oriented based on accounting rules and regulations. Thus financial statements as typically prepared do not provide an "economic" picture and should not be used directly by investors.

Balance sheets typically show equipment and other assets original purchase cost less accounting depreciation. So the first step to look for within the analysis is how account reports are converted into economic financial statements via the process outline in Chapter 6. This is done on a line-by-line basis. The valuation steps must address each asset to develop the complete picture. This asset analysis also will show the owner and others what would be transferred and what would be retained. (As the business owner your review of the steps and the results should be edifying.)

The "normalized" balance sheet has various uses. Do not overlook the important function it serves in determining what assets are, which ones must be part of the "ongoing" business, and which ones are personal and should not be included in any "hypothetical" business sale. (When the day comes to actually market the business, there must be clarity of this nature from the start.)

Let's be sure we are on the same page in the recasting process and the results. One way to think of this process is as if you had a poodle that you hadn't taken to the groomers recently. *(That is the accounting picture.)* It might look like a little sheep. Once taken to a good groomer it might well be revealed to look like a prize poodle. Economic analysis does this to financial statements. It shows an economic picture of the business. As stated this particular activity is called recasting. It is a critical skill for valuators and is important for every business owner to understand. It's not about over or under adjusting. It is a balanced effort to look for the true economic picture of the business.

Once crystallized and clearly presented, this information can be used internally for planning and communicated during an ownership transfer. Recasting takes a lot of work. It takes some good skills. When one first start "grooming" (recasting) the little poodle might not look exactly like a prize poodle. But ultimately recasting work done properly is important to get a picture for planning.

Look at the adjustment for the following actions along with others that may be unique to your business. Accounts receivables adjustments should be properly converted into bad debts. Rents and leases should be based on market values. Since you're looking at the company on a debt-free basis INTEREST-BEARING DEBT is removed. Inventory excesses or overvaluations should be addressed. All cash should be normalized to the level of working capital needed to run the business. What you're looking to transfer is no more and no less working capital than the required balanced amount. It is important to understand that deficiencies in working capital will be a reduction in the value.

Tangible Asset Method

Once completed, this picture of the assets at market value is your first interim value estimate. It is **a tangible asset value.**

Let's look at a simplified example. *(Expanded in Exhibit 2)*

Balance Sheet Components	Book "Value"	Adjustments to: Market Value	Tangible Assets Market Value
Current Assets	1,700,000	-200,000	1,500,000
Fixed Assets	600,000	2,400,000	3,000,000
Total Assets	2,300,000		4,500,000
Current Liabilities	400,000		400,000
Long-Term Debt	1,300,000	-1,300,000	0
Equity	600,000		4,100,000
Total Liab. & Equity	2,300,000		4,500,000

Fixed assets are brought to current market value. These assets were purchased at $6 million and depreciated down to $0.6 million. Analysis shows you could buy used equipment with equivalent capacity and utility for $3 million. Since the valuation analysis is on a debt-free basis, all of the interest -bearing debts in the example are removed at this point. Similarly, the non-operating assets, if any, would be removed as shown.

This analysis provides <u>an interim value estimate for invested capital of $4.1 million.</u> *(This equity entry is highlighted in the example above for easy reference.)* The business may have intangible assets that are not addressed directly in this analysis. To the extent that the intangible assets are generating additional cash flows beyond those attributable to the tangible assets, they will be identified in mass within the income approach.

Let's look at some of the information that is now evident in this beginning analysis:

1. The Working Capital to be transferred is **$1,100,000.**

This computation is the result of the following observations:

Current Assets ($1,700,000) less Excess Working Capital adjustment of ($200,000) are revised to = $1,500,000.

Since Current Liabilities are ($400,000) the Working Capital to be transferred is: $1,500,000 less $400,000. = $1,100,000.

This is the amount of Working Capital that will be targeted for transfer in the hypothetical transaction. In an actual negotiating environment, this point of reference will become an important element in the final deal structured.

2. The Cost Basis for the Fixed Assets is: **$600,000.**

This is the tax basis for the computation of any recapture of tax. *(Recapture of tax is the difference between the original cost of an asset and the cost basis. The tax is at "ordinary income tax rates," the highest rate you will pay. So take a close look at the movement in any allocation that may have attached a different tax treatment.)*

In the example, which we have assumed it to be a Subchapter S Corporation, the original cost of the fixed assets was $6,000,000. The anticipated sale price "at market value" is shown at $3,000,000; therefore, the entire difference between the tax cost basis and the portion of the sale price attributable to the fixed assets ($2,400,000) would be taxed at a "recapture rate." So, if assume the selling business owner's ordinary income tax rate was 30%, the anticipated tax in this transaction at $4,100,000 would be $720,000. *(The gain = $2,400,000 x 30%).*

So, if the assets are sold for $4,100,000 *(this interim value estimate)* and the owner then pays off the Long-term Debt of $1,300,000 and pay $720,000 in income taxes on the transaction the resulting CASH IN HAND would be **$2,080,000.**

Remember: this is just one of several interim methods of valuation that the analyst will apply. The final value estimate has not yet been determined. But, the tax estimate on the transfer (sale) of the fixed assets can be computed. This additional data can be held for a future look at the prospective results. You always want to consult with your tax advisor in any and all situations where taxes are involved. *[Example tax rates used here are just that— "examples".]*

Please note: If your business is currently operating as a "C" corporation, there are significantly different results for an asset sale due to the corporate tax than those shown in this simplified example. Most middle market companies now operate as a "Sub S" corporation or an LLC. If your business has a different entity form, please consult your tax and legal advisors on the advantages and disadvantages associated with operation as "C" corporation prior to a transaction.

This is IMPORTANT! *In this example, if the fixed assets would have shown a market value in excess of $6,000,000 (the original cost), any price achieved above that amount would have been taxed at capital gain rates.*

Consequently, in any actual transaction, the allocation of the final "price" via IRS form 8594 is very important and will be one more thing that will be negotiated between the parties. (Your transaction advisor will carry the weight in the negotiations, but you certainly want to be aware of the tax impact from the allocation process.)

PART 2: INCOME VALUATION ANALYSIS

So how do valuation analysts convert the future benefits of ownership *(future cash flows)* to value? Part of that answer is in an <u>application of the principle of alternatives</u>. *(That is why we took our little diversion tour into these principles.)* The rate of return identified via that principle is the element that attaches the perceived risk of ownership to a particular asset or asset class. *(The part of the valuation analysis will identify the sources or risk and quantify them. This intelligence should be immediately useful within the business's strategic planning process.)*

The report will show exactly how projected cash flow is converted to a value estimate by applying an appropriate "risk adjusted" rate of return. In the marketplace, capital holders can invest in treasury bills on one extreme all the way to venture capital. Capital providers in the graph are shown along a continuum. For business owners, debt and equity capital is provided by banks, asset base lenders, and mezzanine financing groups, private equity groups, personal savings, as well as friends and family on occasion! The rates of return required by the different capital providers is based on the risks they expect to experience.

The simplified chart shows the relative relationship of different capital sources for privately held businesses.

Principle of Alternatives: Function of RISKS

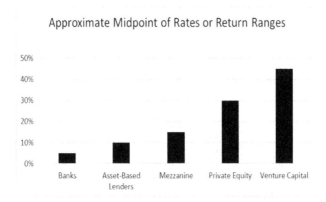

Approximate Midpoint of Rates or Return Ranges

Mezzanine firms do mostly high risk, high rate lending that commercial banks will not do. At times, they will take some limited equity positions. Equity capital comes from personal or corporate savings, friends and family, plus private equity groups (PEGs). PEGs are professional buyers. And venture capitalists are the early stage and/or mid-stage development supporters.

You probably will not see a graph like this in your report ... but you will see the related analysis. The risk rate, which is the output from that analysis, is based on the anticipated uncertainty of the return. The principle of alternatives applies.

This is IMPORTANT!   There is typically a mix of both equity and debt capital within the operating cycles of most businesses. The combination of the component rates or return over time is the enterprises' cost of capital. One of the outputs from a business valuation is identification of the cost of capital for your business. That's the "baseline" hurdle rate you can and should be using in the future for capital budgeting project analysis.

Determining how you might mitigate risks to reduce the cost of capital is part of the value engineering process. Such risk reduction can take many forms within a business. Obviously, as an example, too much customer concentration will increase risks ... both perceived and actual. Risk mitigation is an ongoing management function of considerable importance. The elements and steps that can be observed and acted on will be addressed in a separate section as part of the risk analysis.

Different industries normally exhibit different levels of operating debt. Naturally, these levels may vary due to the characteristics of the industry segment, the maturity of the company, and the risk tolerance of the owners and/or managers.

The risk identified in the rate of return analysis is key to these insights. This discussion is here to provide you with additional background information to help you begin to see what might be done to eventually lower the risk profile for your business.

The development of the risk rate should be clearly developed within the valuation report. You will see that the extended analysis yields a weighted average cost of capital (WACC). This is simply the combination of that part of the capital mix that is debt and the part that is equity.

What you see in this graph is a pictorial analysis over a large group of industries for general reference. Please note there is a flattening out in the area for the mix found in most private businesses. Businesses typically have a debt/equity mix based on MARKET VALUES of each component somewhere between 20 to 60 percent. More debt increases risk and the after-tax cost of capital on a weighted average basis. Additional risks found in a subject business are added by a number of factors.

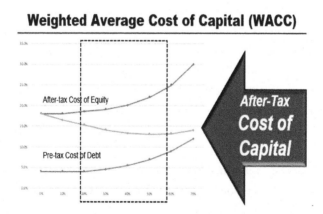

Weighted Average Cost of Capital (WACC)

After-tax Cost of Equity

Pre-tax Cost of Debt

After-Tax Cost of Capital

The valuation analyst is not going to pick a rate from a chart. The analyst will do a complete workup on the systematic and non-systematic risk for your business. Those details and the basis for the judgment used are an important part of the picture you will begin to see of your business.

This chart is a reference to set the stage for your specific review of the rate development in your business valuation report. Observation of the chart shows that the WACC exhibits a flat area that yields rates in the **15 percent to 20 percent after-tax range for many smaller businesses** unless there are unique company equity risk factors that should be applied.

With the <u>addition of these specific company risk factors in the equity component</u>, the WACC for a large number of smaller business may be estimated to be over 25 percent and often near 30 percent. (The WACC for your business may fall within a "typical range" of 15 percent to 25 percent. If it is outside of this range, you should spend sufficient time with your analyst to understand why that is the case!

As noted earlier ... small privately held businesses are like a small ship in a big ocean! Beyond that important observation, the attributes of the business control a buyer's risk assessment. A buyer will look for consistency or inconsistencies of historic performance, dependency on a single customer or vendor, and many other factors. These all impact specific risk.

For example: Let's say you're in the retail furniture business and you have a one major vendor that represented 60 percent of your display floor. This fact could put the business at risk if something happens with that vendor.

The diversification of management responsibility is another area that can add or mitigate some of these risks. Take a periodic look at who's making the major decisions in your company. See who's generating the sales; who's taking care of the critical production areas; and who handles the financial controls that matter. These periodic looks may reveal more than you want to know! A very small group of people may be the key to the success of the business. Consequently, any abrupt change in these key managers can impact the business.

Similarly, product diversification is important. Are you dependent on only one particular product line or do you have multiple product lines in several different market segments? Another risk factor is the operating leverage that you have in the business. That's the gross margin between variable costs and sales. A business generating just 16 percent gross margin is totally different from one with a 36 percent gross margin. Different risks come also from technology change.

Sources of Company Specific Risk

There should also be a keen sensitivity to regulatory and litigation impacts in your industry segment. These are components of non-systematic risk. Systematic risk come from things that happen to all businesses within an industry. The valuation analyst will assess the unsystematic risk that comes from what happens to your individual subject business. Listed below are typical sources of "unsystematic risks." All of these sources should be understood since they will present opportunities to <u>reduce the risk within your business</u>.

You can use this list and other information in your business valuation to identify areas where you can reduce risks!

- *Size (small ship in a big ocean)*
- *Consistency of historic performance*
- *Customer diversification*
- *Vendor diversification*
- *Management responsibility diversification*
- *Product or service diversification*
- *Operating leverage*

- *Technology change sensitivity*
- *Regulatory change sensitivity*
- *Litigation (ongoing or potential)*

In this subject company, the example, we are going to suggest that the analyst found a high degree of risk due to a lack of customer diversification. *(The largest customer is responsible for > 40 percent of total sales.)* This finding would affect the equity rate and will be used within the work shown for reference in the example.

© Michael H Marks

"Ouch, what a blow losing our biggest customer! Think that will screw up the sale of our company?"

If this were your company, the key would be to understand the source of the non-systematic risks and make plans to mitigate them or to at least minimize them.

Please don't get tripped up by the jargon you may see or hear. Non-systematic risks (or sometime the word used is unsystematic*) is simply a term used by appraisers to capture the risks attached to a subject company from its operating profile. These are the risks that go beyond the economic, government, and broader industry risks.*

By doing what you can to reduce known risks, you will directly impact the value of your business. Over time this will better position the business to be attractive to a broader group of potential acquirers.

This is IMPORTANT! <u>A final thought to remember on risk assessments and reduction</u>: **It is the BUYER's perception of risk that counts in a transaction.** It may be different than the market's assessment or even your assessment. *For instance, sometimes, the risk-oriented concerns you have may not be of great significance to a specific buyer. A particular buyer may see the situation differently or believe they have a way to mitigate the subject risks going forward.*

Capitalization of Income Method

Once the income statement is normalized it provides a basis for projecting future earnings. *(This is the REWARD of ownership.)* These projections are used to make an additional interim value estimate. Under the income approach, there are two key metrics: there's the return and the re-rate of return. <u>The return is net after-tax cash flow to invested capital on a debt-free basis.</u>

<u>Investopedia defines "free cash flow" as follows</u>: "Cash a company generates after accounting for cash flows to support operations and maintain the company's capital assets. Unlike <u>earnings</u> or <u>net income</u>, free cash flow is a measure of profitability that excludes the non-cash expenses of the

income statement and includes spending on equipment and assets as well as changes in <u>working capital</u>."

Interest payments (an expense) are excluded from the computation of "cash flow to invested capital" since the analyst is seeing the picture of the operation on a debt-free basis. *(Note: it is always essential in practice to define the "cash flow" that is being discussed, since the cash flow measured varies based on definitions and situations under analysis.)*

<u>The connection between return (free cash flow) and risk is based on the principle of alternatives.</u> We are looking at the rewards of owning a business. That is the future benefit. And we are looking at <u>the risk that the reward is not going to be realized</u>! Analysts may apply different risk adjusted rates of return. These variances are based on their risk assessments. If you absolutely knew you're going to get that return, you would have the same rates of return as Treasury bills. The Treasury rate of return is guaranteed by the federal government. That's not the case in business operations.

The Income Approach to value estimation involves these two key metrics, which you can manage:

- *The anticipated* **REWARD** *(of ownership)*
- *The* **RISK** *that the REWARD will NOT be realized*

That is the way you want to think about the future as you plan and budget. As a business owner, your review of this part of the valuation report will enhance your facility with these two concepts and how they are quantified. Future benefits *(cash flow to invested capital)* could disappear. A risk adjusted rate of return is based on the potential that the reward will not materialize. Both of these measures must be developed through appropriate analysis, which can be replicated by the reader.

Once that is accomplished, the income valuation method or methods may be employed to yield interim estimates of business value.

Future Cash Flow (The Reward)

Recasting analysis and market research provides the basis for income projections. Typically this analysis should be five historic years ... occasionally one may see only three years of analysis. Whatever the time period of the analysis is, it should be sufficient to provide a solid basis for projections. Both industry and company trend analyses are essential to continuously analyze. Trends in all business areas are very important. Those analyses coupled with industry and market research provide the critical basis for income projections from the following inputs:

These elements create the basis for INCOME projections:

- *Five-Year Economic (Recast) Statements*
- *Industry and Company Trends Analysis*
- *Market Research*
- *Company's Strategic/Business Plans*
- *Quality of Earning Analysis*

A major part of developing good income projections for a company is strategy testing. A close look at how competitors are positioned in the market and how business plans are developed is critical. Assessing how management adapts to change is also an important part of the analysis. What analysts are looking for is the future quality and quantity of earnings to get the true economic picture. This vision of the future can be very clouded at times. Ultimately, the valuator will arrive at supportable projections established by analysis, experience, and judgment.

You, as a business owner, want to ask a lot of questions as you look at your own business. A good valuator will ask these questions:

- *How can the business operate most effectively?*
- *Which market segment offers the best opportunities?*
- *When are you going to do certain things?*
- *How can they can be done better?*
- *What can happen?*
- *Who's responsible for what and why?*

The bigger question that underlies all of these queries is this:

- *Will the strategies and plans achieve performance improvement?*

As an owner you should ask these questions over and over again. That is how you <u>develop repeatable processes to generate consistent future revenue growth.</u>

The key step to develop a value estimate is to project the reward. The second step is to quantify the risk that the reward might not be achieved. You can use that information to develop an interim value estimate.

Professional valuators apply what's called the Gordon Growth Model. *(It consists of several variables that the business owner can control.)* The Gordon Growth Model is a model for determination of intrinsic value, based on a future income *(cash flow)* series that grows at a constant rate. Given that income is realized yearly, and the assumption that such income grows at a constant rate into perpetuity, the model solves for the "present value" of the infinite future income stream. *(As such it is a simplified application of the discounted cash flow (DCF) model for a specific situation. The DCF model with be analyzed in a sample application following the Gordon Growth Model examination.)*

Because Gordon Growth Model simplistically assumes <u>a constant growth rate for future cash flows</u>, it is generally only used for companies with projected low-to-moderate growth rates. The more involved DCF model would be used by valuation analysts in situations where the growth rate of cash flows varied by year over time based on a number of variables. However, it is easiest to begin an understanding of "income valuation methods" with a simple example utilizing the Gordon Growth Model to estimate value.

Many business owners know this process as the Capitalization of Income Method.

Before we begin the review of the Gordon Growth Model, let's take a closer look at what constitutes "future cash flow." Where does the cash come from and how does it flow through a business entity? How is it being put to use and how does it eventually provide benefits for the business owner?

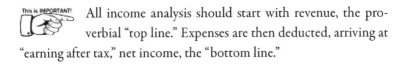 All income analysis should start with revenue, the proverbial "top line." Expenses are then deducted, arriving at "earning after tax," net income, the "bottom line."

Two popular and often discussed income measures are "earnings before interest and taxes" (EBIT) and "earnings before interest, taxes, depreciation and amortization expenses" (EBITDA). Although some people think that these two different lines on the income statement measure cash flow, they don't! The reason they do not measure cash flows is because they do not reflect balance sheet considerations and changes such as working capital needs and capital investments.

Profitable businesses fail if and when they run out of cash. Typically, such results occur when a business has high demands for working capital *(through rapid growth),* increasing capital investments *(to support growth),* and high fixed-debt payments *(to further support growth).* Cash flow computations must include the measurement in all areas directly or indirectly.

Let's look at how the Gordon Growth Model estimates value. This model has three "top level" variables. First is the projection of income measured as future after-tax net cash flow. The income measure is divided by the combination of the second and third "top level" variables—WACC (the risk measure) <u>minus</u> the growth rate.

This is IMPORTANT! The three elements in the equation on the right-hand side of the Gordon Growth Model shows that if you increase the future cash flow you increase value. Or if there is a decrease in the risk you also increase value. Additionally, if you increase the growth rate you increase value. This is the beginning tool business owners can put to work in their business. To the extent that you, the business owner, can impact any of the three variables, you have direct control over the future value of your business. *(As noted, this the story of your business that you can and will create!)*

This is IMPORTANT! As a business owner, you will want to first assess value via your increased understanding of a properly analyzed and presented valuation report ... and second to manage a value increase. In other words, determining how to increase the REWARD of ownership—future cash flows—and decrease the RISK that the future benefits will not be realized!

Let's take a look at a simple example business with projected cash flow for the next year at $1 million. That is "after tax" <u>net cash flow for the business that has accounted for capital equipment investment needs and other capital uses.</u>

Assume an analysis develops a discount rate showing the systematic risk is 15 percent as reflected in the baseline equity rate. To that assessment, the analyst would add the specific (unsystematic risk) for the business to the equity component and bring it through the WACC analysis. Based on analysis, this additional risk factor might add, for this example, 15 percent to the company's equity rate. In this case the revised rate we are going to use is 30 percent. From that equity rate, a market debt rate, and the proper mix of debt and equity, the analyst would develop a WACC for the business. The resulting rate of the WACC for the example company (which we assume had an 80/20 equity/debt mix) is 25 percent. The rate to be applied within the models.

In your valuation report a thorough analysis will have been completed and the present the rate information. *(Your analyst can and should show in the report exactly how the discount rates were developed)*

For this example, it will be stipulated that, based on proper analysis, projected future growth of the cash flow is 5 percent and would be entered into the model with the other two variables. This growth rate has a significant impact on the value estimate, which is why the analyst would have done the industry research and other investigations to be sure there is a solid basis for the projected rate of cash flow growth.

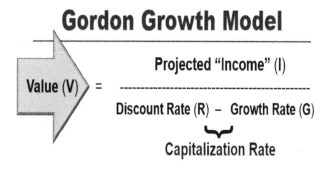

Gordon Growth Model

$$\text{Value (V)} = \frac{\text{Projected "Income" (I)}}{\underbrace{\text{Discount Rate (R)} - \text{Growth Rate (G)}}_{\text{Capitalization Rate}}}$$

Using the Gordon Growth Model, that future cash flow is divided by the discount rate (25 percent) minus the growth rate of 5 percent. The financial community calls the combination of the discount rate and the growth rate the **"capitalization rate."** If we divide the million dollars by the capitalization rate of 20 percent it yields an estimate of value for the business in this case of $5 million. This is the second interim estimate of value for this simplified example. This is one method applied within the income approach as summarized below.

Example: Capitalization Method Math

- Projected cash flow for the "next" year = $1,000,000
- Developed discount rate = 25% (Based on Buildup Rate & WACC Analysis)
- Projected future growth of cash flow = 5%
- Compute the estimated value with Gordon Growth Model.

$$\$5,000,000 = \frac{\$1,000,000}{(25\% - 5\%)} \xleftarrow{} \boxed{\text{After-tax Net Cash Flow}}$$

In most business cases, this is the interim estimating method that will carry the most weight in buyers' decisions.

This "capitalization of income" method gives the valuator and the business owner an interim estimate of value based on the quantifications developed. It should be remembered that these two measures had a number of elements that supported the final determinations.

The example was setup with variables that results in the "proverbial" FIVE TIMES INCOME value estimate for the subject company. That does not make the estimate right or wrong. It must be based on solid analysis to identify the three variables that are the inputs to the model.

$$\$1M \times 5 = \$5M$$

What should be immediately seen is that any such "multiple" is based on a number of hidden elements, which include but are not limited to the following.

- *Equity rate (based on markets and industry info)*
- *Equity rate adjustment for company specific risk*
- *Debt to Equity operating mix*
- *Primary Cash Flow projections*
- *Anticipated Growth of Cash Flow*

What if these underlying elements were different? What would those changes do to the resulting value estimate in this example? This should tell any astute observer that use of "multiples" of "projected income" (not CASH FLOW, as it should be), without knowing the underlying variables is totally inappropriate and will result potentially in value estimates that have little or no "real value"!

To stress this important point! Let's say that management of this subject company had done an exceptional job in reducing risks through diversification, systems building, and so on, and that effective analysis, by an experienced analyst, delivered a WACC of 20 percent versus the 25 percent originally developed.

And ... just to emphasize the impact of these underlying elements, let's look at an extremely different second scenario. This look should show how important is to be sure that effective analysis had taken place.

Let's, for this example, believe that the analysis suggests that the strategic plans, management's strength, and the industry growth factors could give the analyst a lot of confidence that the company could grow cash flows at 10 percent per year for many, many years to follow. This is the "revised" set of inputs to develop an estimate of value!

As you can see in Example 2, these changes resulted in a <u>doubling of value</u> in this example, without any change in cash flow projection for the next year, but by reducing risk and increasing future growth. The example shows that the determination of the growth rate for cash flow must have sufficient analysis and a solid basis for use in any projections.

What we see in practice is that management teams and industry specialists are reasonably effective at projecting growth of revenues for eighteen months to three years. Beyond three years, it take some very solid, added inputs to assert that a "higher-than-normal" industry growth rate will persist. Such information may exist in the form of planned introduction of new products or expansion into a new market. Both of these actions may or may not produce results exactly as planned. Therefore, there is a notable degree of risk associated with such projections.

What if the projection of cash flow for the next year was 20 percent higher ($1.2M)? Right ... that difference would add another $2M to this estimate. <u>So, models do not deliver useful value estimates ... knowledgeable appraisers do</u>! These are the folks charged with the responsibility of properly developing and testing all of the model inputs.

Example 2: Capitalization Method Math

- Projected cash flow for the "next" year = $1,000,000
- Developed discount rate = 20% (Based on Buildup Rate & WACC Analysis)
- Projected future growth of cash flow = 10%
- Compute the estimated value with Gordon Growth Model.

$$\$10,000,000 = \frac{\$1,000,000}{(20\% - 10\%)} \quad \leftarrow \boxed{\text{After-tax Net Cash Flow}}$$

This is IMPORTANT! Consequently, every reader of a valuation report should ask the analyst how the basis for determining the inputs variables was developed and supported. And should also ask what iterations he or she did before settling on the capitalization of income estimate?

As a business owner you want to work with the report so you can do some alternate iterations and assess the impact. This one computation shown in Example 2 highlights the dramatic difference in value estimated as a result of the changes. In practice, the small changes in the business elements that go into the method should be understood and the potential variance in the resulting estimate analyzed. *(These are the changes you, as the business owner, can reasonably make that can dramatically increase the value of your business over time.)*

TAKE ACTION

Small operational improvements can result in significant increases in the value of

YOUR Business!

**"Our seminar today on
Getting Top Dollar for Your Business
will be brief..."**

Discounted Cash Flow

The income method most often used in valuations that have a variation in the future levels of cash flows is the discounted cash flow method (DCF). Like many models, it is relatively easy to outline. In practice it may appear simple; however, it is not always easy to apply effectively. Here are the steps required to apply the DCF model to estimate value for an operating business.

1. Estimate Cash Flow for future periods (five or more years)
2. Determine the Risk-Adjusted Discount Rate
3. Compute the Residual Value at the end of the period
4. Compute the Present Value of future cash flows

5. Sum the "Present Value of the Future Cash Flows" for the discretely estimated period and the present value of the residual value.

This DCF analysis goes back to the original basis for projection of future cash flows. The operating model comes from historic analysis and testing of the relationship of key expenses. In addition to revenue and expense projections, working capital needs to support growth, and the capital investment (CAP-X) requirements are a critical part of the analysis to establish a yearly cash flow, after normalizing the company's expenses. An example of this modeling is provided for reference in Exhibit 4. Please use it only as a basis for working through the model to help you identify the operational drivers that will be presented in your business valuation report. (The model for your business will be different. It will be constructed to replicate the known and planned operating relationships.)

This is IMPORTANT! The valuation analyst should present a detailed workup on the working capital that will be necessary to support operations. This analysis often will take an in-depth look at the "cash flow conversion cycle" for the subject business as well as for a "typical" company in the same industry. This information and industry ratios (WC to Sales) are also often referenced to help assess the future relationship between the level of working capital and projected revenues.

This is IMPORTANT! Similarly, the amount of annual capital investment (CAP-X) may vary widely over the period in which discrete cash flows are projected. These requirements should coordinate closely with the company's strategic plans and assessment of productive capacity maintenance versus capacity expansion. Again, the projection in this area beyond the first five years may rely on industry CAP-X average investments. These are major after-tax uses of cash flow that are discretely estimated or developed with particular metrics.

The reader of a valuation report may see the term "funded depreciation." This is a short cut that an experience analyst may deploy to go from EBITDA to EBIT via cash use in capital investments. It is one way to account for cash uses for ongoing capital investments on a level basis. This may be seen in the underlying analysis before the application of the Capitalization of Income Method or in the residual period for DCF modeling that applies this model to that portion of the DCF analysis.

This technique may also be evident when the analyst is estimating the "maintenance level" of ongoing capital investments ... before any assessment of the amount of capital needed to expand capacity. In short, what the analyst is doing is replacing the "non-cash expense" for depreciation with the "cash used" to purchase the amount of equipment, and so on required to maintain operating capacity. Accounting depreciation is a rules-based entry into the income statement. "Funded Depreciation" is an economic entry to account for the needed annual investments requirements. Often there are industry estimates or history that can temper the analyst's analysis and final determination of the "cash outflow for CAP-X."

A key variable is the "discount rate" used in the DCF model. It is the risk adjusted rate of return developed through analysis. This is in contrast to the "capitalization rate," which is the "discount rate" minus the "growth rate." The yearly cash flow growth in the DCF model is estimated for each year within that part of the analysis. *(Exhibit 4 shows a model for the example company for reference.)*

The "present value" of each cash flow estimate is developed via a discounting methodology. This process should not be a mystery!

For the first period, the risk of not achieving the projected cash flow is one year of "risk." The second year is two years of risk—of not achieving the result, and so on. An example of this "discounting process" is shown here for reflection and new understanding that the process is simply a mathematical way to account for the fact that certain future cash flow projections may not be realized exactly as planned.

Fiscal Year	Adjusted Cash Flow	Discount Rate	Present Value Factor	Present Value	
20X1	1,000	25.0%	0.89	889	[PV = Midpoint Convention]
20X2	1,055	25.0%	0.71	750	[PV = Midpoint Convention]
20X3	1,128	25.0%	0.57	642	[PV = Midpoint Convention]
20X4	1,169	25.0%	0.46	532	[PV = Midpoint Convention]
20X5	1,224	25.0%	0.36	446	[PV = Midpoint Convention]
Terminal Value	5,564	25.0%	0.33	1,823	[Capitalization Rate = 22%]
Present Value of Stream of Benefits				5,081	
Value Estimate Rounded to:				5,000	

The Capitalization rate used to determine the terminal value by the single period capitalization method was 22%]

For you as a business owner, here are two takeaways from your review of a similar chart. First, the 35 percent of the total value estimate comes from the contribution of the terminal value estimate ... done with direct capitalization *(in this example with a 3 percent growth rate)*. Plus, the terminal value estimate before discounts five years hence is about 10 percent above the current value estimate for the business. (Note: working capital adjustments and other similar considerations could be different at that time. Also, the anticipated level of debt could be significantly different than what is currently in the example company. This is useful information for estate and financial planning.)

Obviously, if the adjusted annual cash flows can be increased in each year and the risk rate can be decreased, the value estimate in the future can be notably improved. Those two types of changes do not just happen. They can only be the results of concerted, targeted efforts to achieve different results.

As we finish our review of how income "measures" and "drives" value, here are some thoughts to ponder, remember, and use:

SELLERS: Emphasis the Past ... and Sell the Future
BUYERS: Pay for the Past ... and Buy for the Future

When these analyses and interests intersect, a successful transaction can result for the mutual benefit of the parties.

PART 3: MARKET-BASED VALUATION ANALYSIS

Valuation Using Historic Multiples

THE THIRD APPROACH to valuation (appraisal) is the market approach. In this approach, the analyst will look at historic transactions. To use this approach, it is critically important to be a little skeptical. We hear people refer to historic multiples all the time as if they are the absolute determinant of value. People like to use them because they're simple. But we should be aware of what is happening within these databases.

This is IMPORTANT! Blind use of "market multiples" may be the greatest source of poor price expectation for prospective sellers ... and sometimes for buyers. That is not to say there is no value in this method, if there is proper analysis and a proper application of the data within the valuation process.

Market Approach
(Historic Transaction Data Used to Compare)

Is the subject business = the *"average"* comparable business in the database?

This little graphic suggests dramatic differences between the historic transactions in the databases used by valuation and merger and acquisition analysts. <u>Data is submitted by individuals on a small subset of the total transactions</u>. If you take a more detailed look you recognize variations in the different reported transactions. They may or may not truly compare to your subject business. And your subject business may or may not be average. Is your subject business equal to the average in the databases? Is it better ... much better ... or the reverse?

Consequently, an analyst should refine (segment) the database to get a better picture. Question a valuator who asserts your subject business is equal to the average in the database. It may very well not be comparable!

It is important to be aware that data comes from transaction history. Transactions break down as shown. <u>Only about a third of the ownership changes take place at arm's length</u>. About 15 percent of those deals are handled by brokers who report transaction data to various databases. Businesses transferred to family employees and competitors are typically not reported. About a third of businesses eventually close or disappear from the market and are never transferred.

So we are looking at about 15 percent of one third or may be as small as 4 to 5 percent of total business transactions in the US ... and that is if all the brokers' deals are reported. Given that a lot of brokers do not report transactions, the databases may have as little as 1 or 2 percent of total private sales. So every analyst and every business owner, including you, should be a little bit skeptical, and be careful in how much weight you place on the estimates developed by the market methods. This would be especially true if the market-based estimate varied widely from the estimate with the other two approaches.

What is happening in the market place?

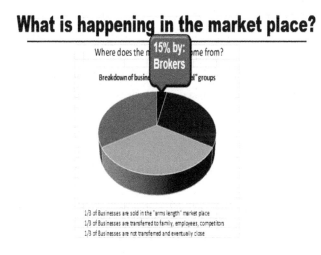

Where does the market information come from?

15% by: Brokers

Breakdown of business "arms length" groups

1/3 of Businesses are sold in the "arms length" market place
1/3 of Businesses are transferred to family, employees, competitors
1/3 of Businesses are not transferred and eventually close

Recognizing that the data available—as presented in the graphic—is very small, doesn't mean we shouldn't use them. We should analyze them and apply them carefully. But as we do put this data to use, we might want to just reflect on these questions!

- *What was the median or mean growth rate of the businesses in the data (revenue and margins)?*
- *What was the source of the underlying average business risk?*
- *How diversified was the customer base?*
- *How diversified was their vendor base?*

- *Which product lines have been strong and Why?*
- *Were there exceptional management teams in place?*

We don't know the answer to these question in the reported transactions within a database and what took place between the parties.

These sales are all at "investment value" in these databases. Collectively, they provide an inference of "fair market value." They do not measure the capital investments required to maintain capacity. Nor the growth rate of the working capital required to support the business. We don't know those key attributes of the businesses in the transactions that were reported. Not knowing those facts should make us skeptical. The market methods are easy to apply to income and revenue. So there is a natural appeal to their use. In this example, we are providing you with an overview of how the market approach is applied and the use of a particular method.

Multiple of Revenue Method

Let's look at the multiple of revenue method. It probably, of the several available methods within the market approach, is the more consistently reported data from historical transactions. In the example, we will use a relationship, as it would have been found direct in the data as the average. The price-to-revenue statistic was shown to be 70 percent of projected revenue based for the industry *(i.e., the database for past transactions showed this to be the statistical average results from those historic deals with sufficient similarity to the subject business. This assumes, of course, that the subject company is directly comparable to the "average" company in the database).*

In our analysis of this business we projected revenue of $7 million. That math (70 percent x $7M) gives us a value estimate of $4.9 million. This is another interim of value estimate based on these two statistics. This process provided a third interim value measurement.

Do Data Bases Report Market Metrics for Industry Multiples ?

Some of the Key Questions for these estimates should be:
1. What is the mean or median growth rate in the data?
2. What are the underlying "average" business risks?
3. What is the CAP-X investment made for the "average" company
4. What is the growth of working capital for the "average" biz?

Multiple of Reve — Example: — Best as Sanity Check

Multiple (70%) of "Revenue" ($7,000,000) = Value Estimate ($4,900,000)

Clearly the market approaches are best used as an overall sanity check for the other two methods. Asset-based methods and income-based methods normally carry more weight. However, when a more extensive analysis of the transaction in the historic database can be performed, the value estimates by these method become more and more relevant in the final analysis.

CHAPTER 10

PART 4: VALUATION ANALYSIS SUMMARY

Reviewing Our AIM Approaches

LET'S LOOK AT a summary of the first three parts to the valuation analysis (process): In the simplified example, we have used an assets-based approach to estimate value of the tangible asset of $4.1 million; we have an income-based approach capitalization of income method estimate of $5 million; and a market-based multiple of revenue estimate of $4.9 million. Once the group of interim estimates are computed, the analyst would do a collective review and assess how they might be used in a willing seller and willing buyer in negotiations within a deal environment. *(The interim estimates in your particular report may be different. What you want to ask is why a particular method was or was not used ... and/or reported.)*

Once each of the estimates are computed, there would be some reflection on how the results should be included in a determination of how the transaction might occur. To replicate the open market, formal or informal iterations on what would happen between buyer and seller are used to make a final assessment. The analyst is seeking what they would and should focus on to draw conclusions.

In many cases, the benefit of the future earnings of the business will take on more importance in any going concern. In many cases, the income approach estimate supported by the asset approach is used to make a final value estimate determination. The analyst is taking AIM at the value. It's not to be a rifle shot. The final value estimate is in the center of the range!

The valuation analyst within the reporting process will use all available information to develop their opinion of value and will state the basis for their opinion. Ultimately, you want to understand this part of the valuation process within any report for your business. As you learn from a report and the discussions with the analyst what the value is today, it is important to look toward what it might be in the future. And how you might directly influence that value. *(This information and new knowledge can make a notable difference in both the strategic and operational business planning process.)*

In this simple example below, with the three interim estimates, the analyst would probably place the most weight on the income method. *(The "real value" is in this understanding: your ability to replicate the process and take action in your business.)*

Reconciliation and Testing of Value Estimate

- Asset-Based Value Estimate (Tangible Asset Method) = **$4.1 M**
- Income-Based Value Estimate (Capitalization of Cash Flow) = **$5.0M**
- Market-Based Value Estimate (Multiple of Revenue) = **$4.9M**

Determine which <u>interim value estimate(s)</u> the market participants would focus on in a hypothetical transaction.

Test the result. Can the new owner purchase the business at the price estimated under "normal" financing terms...and generate positive cash flow? *(Justification for Purchase Test Process)*

In this example, the appraiser (valuation analyst) would conclude that the value of the assets to be transferred is $5 million dollars. *(The value of the INVESTED CAPITAL.)*

This is not the value estimate for the business's equity. That estimate would be developed by combining the invested capital estimate of $5,000,000 and the "excluded assets" of excess working capital of $200,000 to reach a total debt-free estimate of $5,200,000. From this total, the existing long-term debt would be deducted to develop the final estimate of equity value for the business. In this example, that result would be **$3,900,000** ($5,200,000 less $1,300,000).

That is the "fair market value" estimate of the example business, as of the date of the valuation.

FMV of Equity = $3,900,000

It is the value that would be included in an estate filing as the business owner's equity. It is normally the focus of too many people when they quickly review valuation reports. If it is the only purpose for the report, that may be acceptable. But, there is much more information to be secured, including what the picture of a hypothetical transaction would be once crystallized, which is provided for the example company for your review in Exhibit 6.

Let's circle back to the home example to be sure to see this picture clearly. The price for which you sell your home is the total contract amount before the deduction to pay any outstanding mortgage debt. The result of that two-step operation nets you the proceeds (your equity) from the transaction. The same process is used to develop the equity estimate for your business.

Please remember that the Price reference in a transaction is for the "Invested Capital." The "Owner's Equity" is one component of the total capital. The difference between the two is the business's "Interest-Bearing Debt" that must be satisfied.

Justification of Purchase Test

Once these critical comparisons and professional assessments are made and a final value estimate in determined, the next step is to test the ultimate value estimate. This analysis is normally referred to as a "justification purchase test." It should be applied in every business valuation—not to optimize the transaction but to test whether a hypothetical buyer could reasonably make the purchase.

The test is typically presented in reports to give the reader additional insight on just how this $5 million in this particular subject business acquisition might be financed. *(At times the analyst may perform the test within the overall analysis and only report the test results qualitatively.)*

The test, termed "the justification for purchase test," is the analysis that shows whether it is reasonable to expect the buyer to pay that price, support the growth in working capital, and to amortize a purchase with a judicious mix of debt equity. Exhibit 5 provides an example of what this test would look like for the subject business along with a brief explanation of the figures shown in the test result.

Please review this testing example to get a baseline for what it is all about and how it should show in your report. The important information for you, the business owner, is to understand what amount of equity most buyers are providing in transactions and what amount of commercial debt is available.

Banks may lend 2 times cash flow in down markets and up to 3.5 or 4 times cash flow in very positive economic times. Similarly, the amount of equity varies. In a deep downturn, PEGs often put 50 percent equity in a deal ... and at other times the figure might be closer to 30 percent. Given that PEGs will do a recapitalization at times, other variation on the amount of equity in a deal structure may exist. That topic and others of a similar nature are something that this author will address in future books on ownership transition strategies, options, planning, and results.

This is important in the case that you may eventually be presented with what looks like a good buyer. This person or entity may have much less than an optimal amount of equity to use to make a deal. So, if you want to proceed, you may decide to offer some partial financing. Your early understanding of this potential scenario may dramatically impact the terms you might initially offer or need to consider. These situationally specific decisions may add some risk for you ... but may be needed to complete the deal.

In the example company test shown in Exhibit 6, the buyer provided 35 percent equity and borrowed 65 percent of the purchase price from a commercial bank in the amount of $3.25 million dollars. Your new knowledge from looking at the "liquidation value" would have shown that this is very near the limit that a commercial banking underwriter would determine.

OTHER USEFUL INFORMATION

BY TAKING A look at the information from the example, we can highlight some of the key information that every business owner can glean from a report. In this example, this final estimate is $900,000 higher than the tangible assets estimate. So, what additional information does that yield? Simply that the "intangible assets" to be transferred are valued at $900,000. Again, this would become an input to the final allocation of the assets within the $5,000,000 "price" for this hypothetical transaction. *(There could certainly be some movement between fixed assets and intangible assets within the negotiated allocation process. In the example, we used the direct estimate for intangible asset of $900,000.)*

The taxes on the intangible asset portion of the transaction can be computed. Under current tax law (which changes over time) the intangible assets would be taxed at a capital gains rate (in our example, that rate will be applied at 20 percent). Therefore, the additional tax would be $180,000.

This additional information can be utilized by a business owner to compute the <u>after-tax cash</u> for this subject company "as of the date of the value estimate."

Here are the results for the example for an "asset sale":

Selling price = $5,000,000 *(for transferred assets)*
Taxes to pay = $900,000 *(ordinary and cap gain total)*
Long-term debt paid = $1,300,000
Net cash for assets transferred = **$2,800,000**
The excluded assets are retained by the seller:
Excluded assets owned by the business = $200,000
Net cash for transferred and retained assets = **$3,000,000**

This estimate does not include the value of any other excluded assets that would be retained on a personal basis such as artwork or other assets that were never part of the business operation.

Exhibit 6 provides a graphic summary for the transaction of the example company. It, as noted, is simplified. In actual practice you have other assets such as life insurance policies, or securities, or real estate that would be retained. That profile will be the result of many decisions you and your advisors have made over the years.

This is the net cash for investment estimate for use by the financial planner in structuring a future retirement plan, as if it would take place in the current time frame. If a near-term sale is not in the owner's current plans, then the financial planner and the business owner can look further down the road. Those projected "net cash for investment" estimates would be less firm and might replicate what an estate advisor might consider.

The estate advisor would look at the current value estimate of **$3,900,000** ($5,200,000 less the debt of $1,300,000) to begin the discussion on estate planning. There are other items within the report that should be inputs to the estate planning process. One other data point would be the future value of the business hidden in the DCF discounting process.

If the business owners would anticipate holding the business for five years or longer the "terminal value estimate" in the DCF analysis will be of some value. The estate advisor should be able to use this information in formulating applicable early estate planning strategies.

What is not known is the amount of any excess assets or long-term debt that the business may be holding at that future point. Other assets that are individually held and would also be part of the owner's estate should be listed and understood. It is not too late for some strategic estate planning during an exit. But, within the bounds of prudent planning, good professional tax and estate advisors prefer to work well in advance of that day. To do so, they have to operate with the type of data in a valuation report and the and the related uncertainty.

"I can see a bunch of stuff, but I have no clue what it is. ....must be my binoculars!"

> *The big challenge is to become all that you have the possibility of becoming. You cannot believe what it does to the human spirit to maximize your human potential and stretch yourself to the limit.*
>
> *Jim Rohn*

12

Improving Transferable Value

ONCE A "CURRENT value estimate" is reached and the reader (business owner) understands the underlying research and analysis, it is time to assess the current and future situation.

In the simplified business example provided to enhance understanding, different estimates of value were derived; they ranged from $4.1 million to $5.0 million. These estimates were for the "price" of the business, not the owner's after-tax proceeds. In the text and the exhibit, some after-tax net investable cash estimates were developed, as they would be for any specific owner. The owner and his or her advisors would use this information to determine whether the projected cash amounts could be invested to permit the owner to develop a certain level of retirement lifestyle and to meet other family or philanthropic goals.

If the value expected to be realized is not sufficient to meet all the owner's objectives, then a comprehensive plan for the increase in value can and should be developed.

Additionally, the potential impact of an untimely event cannot be fully dismissed. Improving business value and reducing ownership risks by increasing the transferability of the business has several benefits. *(It is the addition of the "readiness" aspect that makes the difference.)* Such steps will position the company to mitigate any unwanted arrival of the Dismal D's in the company's future.

Analysts often refer to seven key attributes that effect value. You will see that the graphic only shows six elements. That is because the business growth measures take two forms that are really significant to the overall value assessments: growth of revenue and growth of operating margins. These two metrics, shown as one larger element in the graphic, should become the targets for continuous and consistent improvement of every privately held business. Professional buyers rank these two elements at the top of their analysis on new prospective acquisitions.

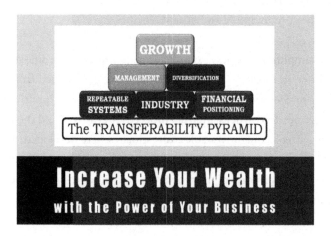

In summary the fundamental determinants of value are as follows:

Growth in revenue and profitability coupled with reinvestment requirements have major impacts on the reward. *(Value is all about RISK and REWARD!)* Increases in each driver within the business's operations impact cash flow and value. Financial leverage can have a mixed outcome. As investment risks and the cost of capital increase, value decreases.

All these key drivers impact the value. Increases in profitability certainly increase value. If things are not on track you will need to take some action to change a strategy and/or change management. It is the business owner's responsibility to do whatever is necessary to make the required changes to keep moving toward a value target.

These primary drivers look at the trends in your business. To take properly timed action you first must look at the reward. What's the benefit of ownership? Then ask yourself, What's the risk that that reward will not be available as anticipated?

Are you doing everything you can do to mitigate the risks and improve the reward? Studying the asset-based methods, the income-based methods, and the market methods will show and reflect what truly happens in the marketplace. People make decisions differently. But they typically are going to focus on the income method.

Most transactions prices are heavily influenced by the income approach analysis. In particular the discounted cash flow method may be applied. This method is used when there is nonlinear future cash flow growth. The method, when used as in the example, can often have a special case of linear cash flow growth. When that occurs, it operates as the direct Capitalization of Income Method.

Many professional buyers use the discounted cash flow method. It is important to know you may see it in a valuation. The capitalization method is simply a specific subset of the discounted cash flow method with linear growth. Understanding the capitalization method provides a solid basis for management and measurement of value. It identifies the three critical valuation variables:

- *Future Cash Flow (the reward of ownership);*
- *Discount Rate (the measure of ownership risk);*
- *Growth in the Reward (increase in the reward).*

If you fully understanding and are using the Gordon Growth Model, work on its three variables: cash flow; risk rate; growth rate. Working on these three alone will provide more than sufficient inputs to start new plans.

Bring this knowledge into your value-planning process. This know-how to improve operations to develop value growth can pay huge dividends by dramatically and consistently increasing value.

The following graphic puts these planning tools into clear perspective:

Fundamental Determinants of Value

Fundamental Value Driver	Change in DRIVER	Impact to VALUE
1. Expected GROWTH in Revenue	Increase	Increase
2. Expected PROFITABILITY	Increase	Increase
3. Expected REINVESTMENT Required	Increase	Decrease
4. Expected FINANCIAL LEVERAGE	Increase	? Depends
5. Investment RISK	Increase	Decrease
6. Comparative COST of CAPITAL	Increase	Decrease

Reward

Risk

This is IMPORTANT! It is good to remember that *price* is what you receive and *value* is what you deliver! *Price* is negotiated. *Value* is based on the various elements of your business. To the extent that you could develop, use, and present key business attributes, you're going to be able to secure a price to match the underlying value!

Planning for and transferring your business is a lot of hard work. It takes some time but can pay huge benefits. To get those benefits, the first step is to understand business valuation and the power of putting it to work in your business.

I trust that this overview has provided enlightenment in that area. So take the next step to increase annual REWARDS (cash flow) and decrease RISKS.

Take action to put your new knowledge to work … so you can increase the future value of your business.

Focus on plans and projects to improve operational performance and increase growth. Work to mitigate risk factors. The key takeaway is that a business valuation can help you focus on development of good systems to manage and measure value. These benefits will help you **increase your wealth through the power of your business.**

A Final Note

Earlier we defined your business valuation report in simple terms as the **"story of your business."** It is the writer's sincere hope that you are now better equipped to create an improved "story of your business's future" based on the information you have learned or will learn from a professional valuation of your business. You really can reach to maximize the business's yearly operating performance and its potential value. Dramatic improvements in both annual free cash flow and future business value can benefit your customers, your vendors, your employees, your family, and your community.

Start Today!
Write <u>the story</u> of your business, "your way," for the future benefit of all involved!

APPENDIX

THE INFORMATION IN these Appendices is provided for reference and use by business owners and advisors. The text and background information has been accumulated over many years from articles, public seminars, and personal interactions with an extended list of valuation experts.

A – Summary of Revenue Ruling 59-60

B – Information Required to Begin a Valuation

C – A Big Misconception about Business Appraisers

D – Extensive Information Found in a Valuation Report

E – Make Financial Reporting Valuable

F – Value Enhancing Books to Read

Appendix A – Summary of Revenue Ruling 59-60

Fair Market Value is considered to represent the value at which a willing seller and a willing buyer, both being informed of the relevant facts about the business, could reasonably conduct a transaction, neither party acting under any compulsion to do so. Court decisions frequently state, in addition, that the hypothetical buyer and seller are assumed to be able, as well as willing, to trade and to be well informed about the property and the market for such property.

Among other factors, Internal Revenue Service Ruling 59-60 provides guidelines for the valuation of closely held stocks. Revenue Ruling 59-60 states that all relevant factors should be taken into consideration, including the following:

1. The nature of the business and the history of the enterprise from its inception.
2. The economic outlook in general and the condition and <u>outlook of the specific</u> industry in particular.
3. The book value of the stock and <u>financial condition of the business</u>.
4. The <u>earnings capacity</u> of the company.
5. The dividend paying capacity of the company.
6. Whether or not the enterprise has goodwill or other intangible value.

Since determining the Fair Market Value of a business is a question, in fact, one must understand the circumstances of each individual case. There is no set formula for the approach to be used that will be applicable to the variety of valuation issues that arise.

Often an appraiser will find wide differences of opinion as to the Fair Market Value of a particular business. In resolving such differences, one should recognize that valuation is not an exact science. A sound valuation will be based on all relevant facts. The appraiser must carefully weigh these facts and determine their aggregate significance.

The Fair Market Value of specific shares of stock in an unlisted corporation will vary as general economic conditions change. Uncertainty about the stability or continuity of the future income from a business will decrease the value of a business in comparison to investments with greater certainty and lower risk. The valuation of shares of stock of a company with uncertain future prospects is a speculative procedure. The judgment must be related to all the factors affecting the company to arrive at a supportable opinion of value.

There is no single accepted formula for determining the Fair Market Value of a closely held corporation; therefore, the appraiser must look to all relevant factors in order to establish the true Fair Market Value as of a given date. In order to establish a uniform system for valuing businesses, the Internal Revenue Service issued Revenue Ruling 59-60 listing the factors to consider in valuing a business.

Appendix B - Information Required to Begin a Valuation

Additional information may be requested to complete the required fuller analysis.

1. <u>Financial Statements for the last five fiscal (or calendar years)</u> and <u>tax returns for the same five-year period</u> along with an internal statement for the most recent month and the corresponding month in the previous year.
2. Summary of Accounts Receivable amounts due on a 30-60-90 Day Basis (i.e., show aging of accounts) as of the end of the last two fiscal years.
3. Opinion as to probable Bad Debts as of latest statement.
4. Outline of Inventory procedures and the Physical Inventories as of the end of the last two fiscal years.
5. Identification of items comprising any Deferred Asset Accounts or Contingency Accounts.
6. Accountant's Depreciation Schedule as of the last two fiscal years.
7. Basis of compensating officers and owners over the last five years.
8. Categorization of current employees by function—Office, Customer Service, Engineering, Maintenance, and so on, plus wage range and rate information by department.
9. Breakdown of Revenues by Major Customers Groups for the last three fiscal years along with a list of the Top Ten Customers by Revenue in each of the past three years.

10. List of insurances carried, claims made in the last two calendar years, and any other pertinent insurance related information.

11. A list of any technical information, trademarks, copyrights, or licenses held by the company.

12. An identification of any government relations that effect the company.

13. A debt schedule that includes all commercial loans and lease agreements.

14. An identification of any other factor that could affect or change the operation in the future, such as a major equipment purchase or the loss of key personnel and/or customers.

15. A copy of the present Workmen's Compensation rating information.

16. A copy of the present Unemployment Compensation rating information.

17. List of all underground and aboveground storage tanks by type, size, and use.

18. Copy of all real estate and equipment appraisals completed within the last five years.

19. A summary of any pension plan and the annual benefit valuation summary for each officer or owner who is a participant in the plan.

20. A copy of all buy-sell, option, or consulting agreements.

21. A complete list of all ownership interests and the relationship of these parties, along with all transaction history for the past ten years.

22. A copy of the Corporation's by-laws and the most recent business plan (formal or informal).

Appendix C – A Big Misconception about Business Appraisers

One of the biggest, but wholly understandable, misconceptions that attorneys and clients have about business appraisers is that appraisers must have prior experience with the type of business, geographic region, and nature of the circumstances involving the business to be appraised.

These concerns often arise in cross-examination, as well as in initial interviews with prospective clients. Both parties are naturally concerned about appraisal expertise and familiarity with a given business, industry, region or valuation context. The point is that although an appraiser may <u>not</u> have previously appraised a business with identical circumstances, his or her experience with similar businesses and situations is eminently applicable. Ultimately, fair application of the business value principles and effective analysis of the facts and circumstances unique to the businesses current position and future prospects is what is important.

<u>**Qualified appraisers have four essential skill sets**</u>:

1. Economic and industry research and analysis
2. Qualitative and quantitative company analysis
3. Accounting, tax, legal and regulatory knowledge
4. Technical valuation ability

An industry consultant, accountant, or broker with no appraisal training is not qualified to handle issues of the fourth type, such as the standard and level of value, the valuation date, and appropriateness of alternative valuation approaches and methods. These considerations are critical to the development of a sound appraisal.

A qualified appraiser is required by professional standards to obtain the knowledge and skills of the first three types in order to undertake an assignment. Credentialed, peer-reviewed appraisers have demonstrated competency in these vital areas. They know what questions to ask and who to ask them in order to obtain necessary information. *(This is how they achieve a result that is documented in your valuation report that is truly full of "real value" to improve planning for your company's future.)*

Therefore, if you want to have YOUR business valued, leave no stone unturned to retain an Accredited Appraiser.

Ask for references and discuss similar assignments to assure that you have the best professional for your business needs! Think of the business valuator (appraiser) as a member of your advisory team. Someone you can rely on over the years to help with a variety of valuation issues as you formulate personal, business, and estate plans.

Appendix D – Extensive Information Found in a Valuation Report

What can a business owner, or their advisors, learn directly or indirectly from a business valuation report?

The following list provides a broad look at the information that is normally directly highlighted in the report or part of the analysis performed by the valuator. Not all of this information will be addressed or referenced in every report. However, most of this information will be indirectly considered if not formally reported. Look for this information, add it to your personal knowledge, and put it to use to enhance the value of your business.

- *Analysis of historic earning power*
- *Analysis of the general economy*
- *Analysis of the industry (or industries)*
- *Analysis of the regional economy*
- *Assessment of Porter's Five Forces Framework*
- *Basis for projected growth*
- *Cost basis of potential gains for tax computation*
- *Company organization*
- *Company specific risks*
- *Competitor analysis*
- *Contracts in place*
- *Copyrights*
- *Cost of capital for investment decisions*
- *Cost of corporate equity*

- *Customer concentration assessment*
- *Customer turnover*
- *Distribution methods*
- *Employee turnover*
- *Estimate of tangible assets value*
- *Estimate of intangible asset value*
- *Estimate of invested capital*
- *Estimated tax impact of a hypothetical transaction*
- *Excess or deficiency in working capital*
- *Expectations for seller financing requirement*
- *Fair market value of rental/lease rates*
- *Fair market value of real estate (from separate report)*
- *Government regulatory impact*
- *Government legislation impact (current/future)*
- *Identification of assets to be retained*
- *Industry ratios for comparison*
- *Leases in place*
- *Licenses required and in place*
- *Long-term project cash flow growth (basis)*
- *Management team assessment*
- *Management responsibility diversification*
- *Marketing methods*
- *Most probable selling price*
- *Net cash to seller at closing*
- *Net cash to seller in transaction*
- *Ownership distribution*
- *Patents in place and in use*
- *Prior sales of corporate stock*
- *Projected growth of revenue (basis)*
- *Projected net cash flow to invested capital*
- *Proprietary processes*
- *Proprietary products*
- *Recapture tax estimate*

- *Risk factor for the business*
- *Seller financing anticipation (impact)*
- *Systems and procedure in place (missing)*
- *Tax basis for individual assets*
- *Technology in use and impact*
- *Trade secrets*
- *Typical future financial arrangements*
- *Vendor analysis (cost and other elements)*
- *Vendor diversification impacts*
- *Weighted-average cost of capital*

Appendix E - Make Financial Reporting "Valuable"

You should by now have an enhanced appreciation of the formal valuation process and the volumes of information that can be developed and used to improve business value. You can use these concepts, which can be historically applied, to periodically calculate a value for your business in between formal valuations. These results should provide a consistent measure to assess your progress in managing and increasing the value of your business.

Since the inputs to any such valuation analysis are from the company's financial statements, it is possible to employ those materials to develop "value information" for these uses:

- *Shareholder Buy-Sell Agreements*
- *Profit-Sharing Arrangements for Key Employees*
- *Benchmark Reporting to Investors or Stakeholders*

The value measure might exhibit an "Agreed-Upon Value" and differ, in a known manner, from a fair market valuation value estimate. The use and purpose for this value data point should control any deviations from a standard value definition.

For example, the parties could agree on a "value" based on a specific Fair Market Value analysis or an "Agree-Upon Value" and use the financial accounting system to provide adjustments over certain periods of time. An adjustment might be made for the direct amount of change in the business's working capital or last-in-first-out reserves. Or, it may factor in, or exclude, receipts from an insurance policy's costs or proceeds. Development and formalizing use of such an approach to benefit the shareholders and for a stated purpose should be accomplished only with the advice of your business valuator, accountant, and attorney.

Every company has its uniqueness. Consequently, the financial reporting system should be designed to provide a variety of information on everything from direct operating history to loan covenants, liquidity, and valuation. These key measures should be compared to history as well as tracked and trended to assure the best information is delivered on a periodic basis by the "extended" financial reporting system. That is how you can "celebrate and recalibrate" the direction of your company.

Appendix F - Value-Enhancing Books to Read

Strategic Learning: How to Be Smarter Than Your Competition and Turn Key Insights into Competitive Advantage

Willie Pietersen [**ISBN 978-0-470-54069-5**]

Excellent process development strategy for small and mid-sized business owners to apply daily.

All the successful business owners I have had the opportunity to work with in the sale of their businesses have one key attribute ... they never stopped learning. Some had the benefit of extensive formal education while others did not. Regardless of the foundation, they all continuously strived to learn more and more about their business, their industry and their competitors. This book helps systematize that important process for business leaders.

Value Planning: The New Approach to Building Value Every Day

Lawrence B. M. Serven [**ISBN-0-471-438103**]

Of all the books that have been published on planning, this book has the most effective, practical treatment of the subject. Planning is a process that can create fantastic results. Just one strategic change at the right time can propel a business and the value of the business to great heights.

This book provides a simple "hands-on" approach. The self-diagnostic measures are especially useful in assessing organizational progress. This really is a blueprint for creating shareholder value through the careful development of management systems.

Basic Business Appraisal

Ray Miles [**ISBN-0-471-88555-X**]

This book was written for both the beginner and the experienced business appraiser. It is appropriate for study by any interested business owner.

This is a text that provides some solid theory to enhance understanding of the principles of alternatives and substitutes. It follows a logical progression, beginning with basic concepts and continuing through the appraisal process. This text is for the business owner who really wants to create a solid foundation in business appraisal knowledge as a means to increase the value of her/his business. This book is currently not in print. However, there are copies in most business libraries.

EXHIBITS

1 – Graphic Summary Transaction Template

2 – Example Company: Balance Sheet

3 – Example Company: Income Statement

4 – Example Company: Discounted Cash Flow (DCF)

5 – Example Company: Justification for Purchase Test

6 – Example Company: Graphic Deal Info Summary

Exhibit 1 – Graphic Summary Transaction Template

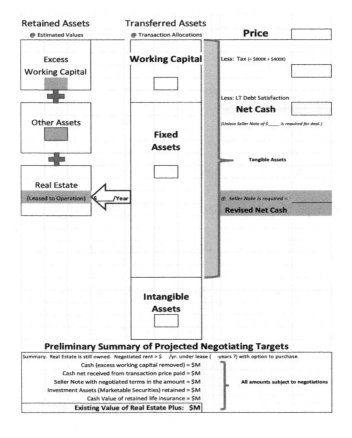

This template is shown to provide a view of the information that can be gained regarding a potential future transaction based on the information in the valuation report. The assumption is that the real estate used in the business will be leased from the owner to the operating entity. The balance of the template is laid out to show where different information can be entered to develop a complete picture of a hypothetical transaction ... as of the date of the valuation.

To further the understanding of how to use this template, the simplified information from the example company will be entered for reference.

If the information in the summary transaction template was all that you could glean from a valuation report beyond the individual "value estimate," it would be well worth engaging a professional to do the work. But, as you have learned in this book, there is much, much more actionable information within the valuation (appraisal) report for you to use.

Exhibit 2 – Example Company: Balance Sheet

This is the very simplified example of a company's balance sheet with limited accounts entries just sufficient to show the recasting process.

Balance Sheet Components	Book "Value"	Adjustments to: Market Value	Tangible Assets Market Value
Cash	300,000	-200,000	100,000
Accounts Rec'b	600,000		600,000
Inventory	800,000		800,000
Current Assets	1,700,000		1,500,000
Equipment	5,600,000		
Vehicles	400,000		
Fixed Assets Cost	6,000,000		
Depreciation	5,400,000		
Fixed Assets	600,000	2,400,000	3,000,000
Total Assets	2,300,000		4,500,000
Current Liabilities	400,000		400,000
Long-Term Debt	1,300,000	-1,300,000	0
Equity	600,000		4,100,000
Total Liab. & Equity	2,300,000		4,500,000

As noted previously, this book's purpose is to advise the reader on the vast amount of useful information in a valuation. One place to look closely is in the "recasting" of the historic balance sheets and income statements. This recasting—adjustments to an economic picture—is a critical application of professional knowledge and good industry research. It will show the historic financial position of the business.

Each adjustment made by the analyst would be based on analysis and comparative references. In this simplified example company, there are only three adjustments within the company's balance sheet:

1. Working Capital Adjustment
2. Fixed Assets Adjustment
3. Long-Term Debt Adjustment

Working Capital Adjustment

The analyst would do extensive work in this area to determine the proper amount of working capital needed to effectively operate the company. Such analysis might include a full review of the cash conversion cycle as well as of a comparison with other industry participants, and putting some weight on the industry ratio of working capital to sales (6:1). In this example, it would have been determined that the required working capital would be $1,100,000, and would necessitate the separation of $200,000 of current assets *(in this case, cash)* as an "excess asset" that can be added back to the entity value.

This is IMPORTANT! Understanding of how and why working capital was adjusted in the valuation is very important because in that "someday transaction" you will be participating in, the amount of working capital transferred will be the subject of serious negotiations. You want to transfer the level needed for the business to proper operation ... no more.

Fixed Assets Adjustment

The fixed assets (equipment, machinery, and vehicles) would be adjusted in the example from the book value to the appraiser's estimate of market value. In this case, the market value in total was determined to be $3,000,000 so the adjustment from book value is $2,400,000. (This difference will become important in the eventual tax estimated within a hypothetical transaction.)

Long-Term Debt Adjustment

The objective in the interim valuation steps of the process is to determine the value of the "invested capital" for the business. This is the value on a debt-free basis ... so the adjustment is made as show, in the example to remove the long-term (all interest-bearing) debt to develop the interim estimate for the tangible assets within the business.

The analyst would normally develop a Liquidation Value Estimate for inclusion in the report. If the Liquidation Value was not shown directly, the estimate can be developed with some additional analysis.

In this simplified example company, the inventory might be $200,000 less than market value under a liquidation scenario. Similarly, the fixed assets might be $600,000 less, resulting in a Liquidation Value estimate of: $3,300,000. *(This type of analysis is normally subject to wider swings and differences of opinions. For this example, it is shown here only to provide the reference for the Justification of Purchase Test lending limit.)*

Exhibit 3 - Example Company: Income Statement

This is the very simplified example of a company's income statement with limited accounts entries just sufficient to show the recasting process.

- YEAR -	CY 20X0		CY 20X0
Income Statement Components	Accounting Statement	Adjustments to: Market Value	Economic Statement
Sales	6,800,000		6,800,000
COGS	4,450,000		4,450,000
Gross Margin	2,350,000		2,350,000
Sales Expense	500,000		360,000
Rent Expense	160,000	-15,000	145,000
Owner's Salary & Benefits	250,000	-100,000	150,000
Other Admin. Expenses	95,000		95,000
Total Operating Overhead	1,005,000		750,000
EBITDA	1,345,000		1,600,000
Depreciation Expense	220,000	-70,000	150,000
EBIT	1,125,000		1,450,000

Expense Adjustments

The various adjustment to example company's historic income statement are shown. All such adjustments would be made to provide an economic statement with each expense shown as an estimate of "fair market value." Some companies do not require many adjustments.

The analyst will look carefully at each expense and make the necessary determinations.

Depreciation Adjustment

Depreciation within the original financial statement is a non-cash expense. Some analysts will make an adjustment in this line item to move the result to "funded depreciation." This would be the amount of capital expenses that the analyst determined would be required each year to maintain the operating capacity in place. (By using this technique, the analyst can develop an EBIT *(earnings before interest and taxes)* estimate that is a true simple cash flow entry ... for use in the further analysis.)

Taxes and Working Capital Considerations

Please note that this recast picture only goes through EBIT. And we know EBIT is not "net cash flow." There are taxes to be paid and deducted as well as accounting for the cash use for additional working capital. All of these variables must be projected to establish a base year for analysis.

Since the CAP-X in the EBIT development was "funded" (i.e. cash outflow), the math to determine the cash flow for the Capitalization model is as follows:

EBIT (Earnings before Interest and Taxes) =	**$1,475,000**
Less: Taxes @ 30% =	442,500
Less: Working Capital Increase =	33,000
After-Tax Cash Flow to Invested Capital =	**$1,000,000**
	(Rounded)

Exhibit 4 provides an analysis that shows this development in the column under 20X1. You will see in that exhibit that the reduction in cash from taxes and working capital use yields a "cash flow to invested capital" estimate of $1,000,000. This is the same "next year" analysis result for both DCF and the Capitalization of Income models.

This "recasted income statement" provides the analyst with a sound basis for future projections of cash flow for the company. The recasting skill is one of great importance for both business valuators and transaction advisors since similar future economic income statement presentations will also be the basis of part of the negotiations in a future sale.

Exhibit 4 - Example Company: Discounted Cash Flow

This discounted cash flow (DCF) exhibit is provided strictly for reference. This book has not endeavored to teach the actual valuation process, but rather how to get the most value from a valuation report.

	20X0	20X1	20X2	20X3	20X4	20X5
Annual Inflation Rate →		3.0%	3.0%	3.0%	3.0%	3.0%
Real Growth Rate →		0.0%	4.0%	0.0%	2.0%	0.0%
Calendar Year of Operation	20X0	20X1	20X2	20X3	20X4	20X5
	Adj. Actual					
Sales Revenue	6,800	7,000	7,490	7,715	8,100	8,343
Direct COGS (Basic)	3,400	3,500	3,745	3,857	4,050	4,172
Indirect COGS (Basic)	750	800	840	865	900	927
Cost of Goods Sold	4,150	4,300	4,585	4,723	4,950	5,099
Gross Margin	2,650	2,700	2,905	2,992	3,150	3,245
G & A Expenses	690	700	721	743	773	796
Selling Expenses	360	375	411	434	467	493
S, G & A Expenses	1,050	1,075	1,132	1,177	1,239	1,289
Operating EBITDA	**1,600**	**1,625**	**1,773**	**1,815**	**1,911**	**1,956**
Economic Depreciation = Cap X	150	150	150	150	150	150
Adj. Operating Income - EBIT	1,450	1,475	1,623	1,665	1,761	1,806
Interest on LT Debt	75	75	75	75	75	75
EBT	1,375	1,400	1,548	1,590	1,686	1,731
Taxes @ 30%	413	419	464	477	506	519
EAT	963	981	1,084	1,113	1,180	1,212
Plus: Int. Net of Tax Deduction	53	53	53	53	53	53
CAP-X for Capacity Increase	1,000	0	0	0	0	0
Less: Incr. in Working Capital	Base Year	33	82	37	64	41
Cash Flow to Invested Capital		**1,000**	**1,055**	**1,128**	**1,169**	**1,224**

In the case where the analyst developed a discounted cash flow analysis, the reader should take the time to understand how the DCF model was constructed and how it was tested.

Here the first year (20X1) is discretely projected with the analysis and budgeting by the subject company. In this example, for the remaining years shown, you can see that the Direct COGs were estimated at 50 percent of sales revenue and that the Indirect COGs were estimated at the inflation rate plus half of the growth rate. Relationships of this type would be developed and used for each group of expenses.

You can see in the example that the "cash flow to invested capital" is increasing each year at 5 percent (a linear relationship). If this were the actual cash, the DCF model would probably not have been employed. The DCF model is useful in capturing future projections that vary year to year. The benefit to the report reader is be able to understand the model in a manner sufficient to assess how various operating changes would impact future cash flows. The power, for the business owner, is to recognize how much the value estimate would change with faster growth; lowering COG; constricting increase in overhead categories; and more.

If you take the time to uncover and understand the value drivers in your business, you will be well on the way to enhancing value over time.

Exhibit 5 – Example Company Justification for Purchase Test

This is a test to show that, under normal financing conditions, a buyer could complete a transaction and pay off the loan or loans in a reasonable period of time.

ALL DOLLARS IN $(000)		Year 20X1	Year 20X2	Year 20X3	Year 20X4	Year 20X5	Total
(YEAR AFTER ACQUISITION OF OPERATIONS)							
Adjusted Income * EBITDA		1,625	1,773	1,815	1,911	1,956	9,081
New Expenses:							
Depreciation (Non-economic)	1	400	400	400	400	400	2,000
Interest - Note #1		163	133	102	70	36	504
TAXABLE INCOME		1,062	1,240	1,313	1,441	1,520	6,577
Income Tax Rate @ 30%		319	372	394	432	456	1,973
NET INCOME (Corp.)		743	868	919	1,009	1,064	4,604
Principal - Note #1	2	588	618	648	681	715	3,250
NET available for:		555	650	671	728	749	3,354
WC addition, CAP-X, or distribution							
CAP-X Estimate (Funded)		150	150	150	150	150	750
Anticipated WC Additions	3	33	82	82	82	82	360
Net available for distribution		372	419	440	496	518	2,244
Or...Reinvestment in the company							

In our example, you see that this is possible with a 35 percent equity portion for the purchase price capital. The example shows that the buyer might be able to complete the purchase with slightly less equity. One could also argue that the price could be higher. However, it should not be forgotten that this example company has a high degree of risk due to the lack of customer diversification.

The justification purchase test does not endeavor to optimize a transaction structure. Rather its use is to generally test the estimate of value *(price)* under "normal financing" terms and conditions. It is useful to provide the reader with the knowledge that the value estimate for the company, net of excluded assets, is in the right range.

Professional buyers will use this simple spread sheet to test the results for "quick look" scenarios. One example might be a test to see if the business will still provide positive cash flow with a decline of 20 percent or more in EBITDA. This is part of the prudent planning any buyer would undertake to develop contingency plans for an uncertain future.

Exhibit 6 - Example Company: Graphic Deal Info Summary

This is the "deal summary" for the example. It provides the information from the report on one page for reference.

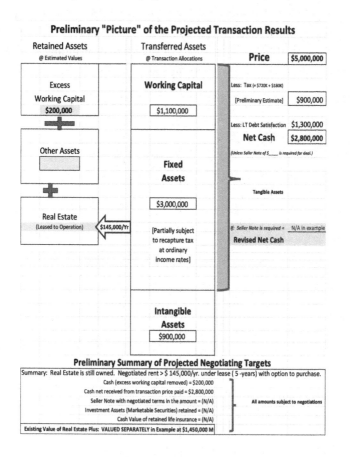

Preliminary "Picture" of the Projected Transaction Results

Retained Assets	Transferred Assets	
@ Estimated Values	@ Transaction Allocations	**Price** $5,000,000

- Excess Working Capital $200,000
- **Working Capital** $1,100,000
- Less: Tax (= $720K + $180K) [Preliminary Estimate] $900,000
- Less: LT Debt Satisfaction $1,300,000
- **Net Cash** $2,800,000
- *(Unless Seller Note of $____ is required for deal.)*
- Other Assets
- **Fixed Assets** $3,000,000
- **Tangible Assets**
- Real Estate (Leased to Operation) $145,000/Yr
- [Partially subject to recapture tax at ordinary income rates]
- *If: Seller Note is required =* N/A in example
- **Revised Net Cash**
- **Intangible Assets** $900,000

Preliminary Summary of Projected Negotiating Targets

Summary: Real Estate is still owned. Negotiated rent > $ 145,000/yr. under lease (5 -years) with option to purchase.

Cash (excess working capital removed) = $200,000	
Cash net received from transaction price paid = $2,800,000	
Seller Note with negotiated terms in the amount = (N/A)	All amounts subject to negotiations
Investment Assets (Marketable Securities) retained = (N/A)	
Cash Value of retained life insurance = (N/A)	
Existing Value of Real Estate Plus: VALUED SEPARATELY in Example at $1,450,000 M	

From this simplified example company summary, you can see that the information developed with the report shows the owner, in a hypothetical transaction, would have $3,000,000 in cash from the sale. The total cash is the sum of $2.8M from the deal, plus the retained excess working capital of $200K.; a real estate lease for five years at $145,000 per year; and still retain ownership of the real estate with a value of $1,450,000. *(This is the input information that is needed by the financial planner to assess the match with your future living requirements. And, it is part of the input for your estate attorney.)*

If there is a gap between what the net cash and the other assets owned will produce in the future, it would be time to go back and determine a value target for the business that would fill this gap ... and work to get there.

ACKNOWLEDGEMENTS

IN ALMOST EVERY book, the author thanks individuals who were most instrumental in helping him or her develop and complete the book. There are a few folks who must be named due to their direct or indirect contributions. This book is no different in that regard.

I would like to thank a young English major who motivated me to learn to write a long time ago, and two early mentors who taught me that the best way to address bureaucratic friction is to focus on the underlying truth and facts. I am constantly assisted from hearing these two individuals, Phil Gregory and William Yukanavich, in my ear. They taught me and many others how to get things done in the right way for the right reasons. This book, which in this manner is similar to my international best-selling book, *When is the Right Time to Sell My Business?*, reflects that fundamental action-oriented approach.

My new editor, whom I couldn't write without, knows more about written communications than most English professors. She has made the difference in getting this book into your hands. I want to thank her for doing the best she could with an engineer-turned-author to improve this book for your benefit.

My family members who have supported me and permitted me to free the time to complete this project. My wonderful wife is a "teacher's teacher." The structure of the book is a direct reflection of the educator approach she brings to every task. I am thankful for her sharing many teaching fundamentals that are employed herein to help facilitate the flow and emphasis required to try to transfer knowledge.

There are many, many other people to thank who have helped me over my varied career. This list varies from the sponsors of the many valuation seminars I have been privileged to present, to the founders of the Institute of Business Appraisers and other professional organizations. What is offered for consideration in this book was learned from these valuation and transaction advisors as well as from many clients. I will always be thankful for the up-close view of how consummate professionals and inspired business owners manage their businesses to increase wealth over time.

OTHER RESOURCES

MICHAEL MARKS is a masterful cartoonist and an expert in database marketing. His years of intermediary experience give him the insight required to craft the cartoon graphics included in this book. You can access Mike and his extensive direct marketing skills at

toonsandtips@richmark.biz
www.ToonsandTips.com or **www.Nation-List.com**

MERGERMENTOR.COM is "the" educational website designed for business owners interested in professionally preparing and selling their businesses. It provides valuation information, transaction articles, checklists, and planning templates for use in the process. This is the place to add knowledge on how to sell your business quickly and quietly at the right time for the right price.

And ... registration is now FREE for Business Owners! Please go there and learn all you can.

WWW.MERGERMENTOR.COM

is the Trusted "Must Have" Resource

for Business Owners Around the World

Merger Mentor is your one-stop online platform that makes valuing and selling your business stress-free, effortless and ensures you sell at the right time, to the right buyer, for the right price. Inside you'll get instant access to all this:

- *Proven performance enhancement strategies you can use to increase the value of your business fast.*
- *Easy-to-use business valuation methods so you can find out what your business is worth right now in today's market.*
- *Checklists, templates, and resources for getting your business ready for sale, optimizing how much it's worth, and preparing you for the transaction.*

And that's just a fraction of what's waiting for you, there's much, much more! Merger Mentor gives you the most up-to-date, relevant, and actionable information to help you sell your business for the maximum amount in the minimum length of time.

To become a member of Merger Mentor, Go to the Link Below

www.MergerMentor.com

(FREE Access for Business Owners)

ABOUT THE AUTHOR

RICHARD MOWREY is an expert in the valuation and sale of privately held businesses with a reputation for getting the job done quickly and quietly, at the right price. He has shown countless business owners how early access to comprehensive, easy-to-use information can be effectively applied to dramatically increase the value of their businesses.

Richard's first book, *When Is the Right Time to Sell My Business?* was recognized as a #1 international best seller. One of the three expert answers to that title question (provided in depth in that first book) is "When the business is ready." This second book endeavors to provide the reader with some additional tools and techniques to help improve performance to get a business ready for sale through knowledgeable use of a business valuation report.

Richard has owned and operated four businesses, and bases his books on the knowledge he acquired from over forty years spent as both a business owner and a hands-on ownership transition advisor. He has been an active member of the board of directors of many businesses and has a wealth of knowledge and practical experience.

Richard has had various direct management responsibilities in public companies and private enterprises, in addition to proficiency in start-up companies and turnaround situations. He has decades of experience in business valuation and ownership transfer issues found in the private market. He is well-known for his unique ability to easily navigate complex valuation and business sale issues. He has gained a unique combination of experiences from counseling businesses in transition, which prompted the development of seminars and the specific educational materials targeted for business owners. This material can be found at **www.MergerMentor.com.**

Richard is a sought-after speaker on valuation and ownership transfer topics. He has presented educational courses in valuation and transactional planning, and has taught at Wentworth Institute of Technology, Rollins College, and Indiana University of Pennsylvania, as well as for the International Business Brokers Association (IBBA), and the M&A Source, which is the largest international organization of business intermediaries.

Richard is a Fellow of the IBBA and has held, during his long career, the following certifications: Certified Management Accountant (CMA) from the Institute of Certified Management Accountants, Certified Business Appraiser (CBA) from the Institute of Business Appraisers, and Certified Business Intermediary (CBI) from the International Business Brokers Association as well as other certification and designations. He holds a BS in Mechanical Engineering and an MS in Management Science from Rensselaer Polytechnic Institute.

HOW TO CONTACT THE AUTHOR

FOR FURTHER INFORMATION or to contact the author regarding a speaking engagement, please visit www.RichMowrey.com or call Richard Mowrey directly at **(814) 938-8170.**

Please visit www.PrioritySeminars.com for seminar planning materials. For information on other professional services, please contact your local experienced advisors.

www.RichMowrey.com

A REQUEST

I WROTE THIS book to help business owners acquire the ability to gain a lot of knowledge from a business valuation and to prepare for the most important transaction in their business careers. I trust it has done that for you. If so, would you please leave a review on Amazon to help other business owners gain from the important content in this book?